LIVING TO PROWL

ALSO BY SAM PICKERING

LIVING TO PROWL

Sam Pickering

The University of Georgia Press

Athens and London

AC
8
P665
1997

Published by the University of Georgia Press

Athens, Georgia 30602

© 1997 by Sam Pickering

All rights reserved

Title page illustration © 1997 by Wendell Minor

Book design by Sandra Strother Hudson

Set in Berkeley Old Style

Printed and bound by Maple-Vail

The paper in this book meets the guidelines for
permanence and durability of the Committee on
Production Guidelines for Book Longevity of the
Council on Library Resources.

Printed in the United States of America

01 00 99 98 97   C   5 4 3 2 1

Library of Congress Cataloging in Publication Data

Pickering, Sam, 1941–

Living to Prowl / by Sam Pickering

p. cm.

ISBN 0-8203-1940-6 (alk. paper)

I. Title.

AC8.P665   1997

081—dc21   97-18691

British Library Cataloging in Publication Data available

CONTENTS

LIVING TO PROWL

MY SUMMER VACATION

In March I visited Uncle Coleman in Houston. Four years ago Coleman's wife, Amanda, died, and he lived alone. Although Coleman was eighty-four years old and I was his only living relative, I had not seen him in twenty-nine years. After Amanda's death Coleman rarely left his house, and for the past three years his yard man brought him food. Recently, hucksters had begun to prey upon Coleman, convincing him to purchase stock in gold and titanium mines, buy tickets in lotteries in Germany and Hong Kong, and donate money to dubious conservative organizations. As a result Coleman lost his savings. With an income of less than thirteen thousand dollars a year, he did not have enough money to keep himself and a house. Coleman lived in a back room, spending days curled in bed dozing, getting up only to eat cereal and cookies. He slept in his clothes, and during the week I spent in Houston, he changed only when I dressed him. When I asked a question, he usually said, "I can't remember. I'm too old." Coleman blamed hospitals for Amanda's death and refused to see doctors. Three years ago while I was in Australia he collapsed. A neighbor drove him to a hospital and discovered he was starving. For a while the neighbor supplemented the food supplied by the yard man. But the neighbor was also old, and after Coleman rejected help from charities, such as Meals-on-Wheels, she stopped cooking for him.

Coleman was wasting away, and when I was in Houston, I force-fed him, buying gallons of ice cream and taking him to restaurants. Clearly, Coleman could not manage life, and in hopes of raising money for him I obtained power of attorney and put his house up for sale. When I left Texas in March, I promised to return during the summer and find him "a nice place" in which to live. As summer approached, however, I dreaded going to Texas. I fretted about bills and taxes, selling furniture, and paying for a nursing home. Coleman's house hung on the market, and because I paid his expenses until the house sold, monetary concerns nagged me. Often I woke at three or four o'clock at night agitated by worry. I telephoned Coleman every Sunday in the spring, but then three weeks passed and I did not telephone, unconsciously hoping, I suppose, that if I separated myself from his voice, he would vanish. Of course, not calling made me feel guilty. Several times Vicki asked what we would do once we arrived in Houston. I hadn't formed plans. Instead of answering Vicki I took the dogs for walks in the woods, imagining that amid the new leaves troubling questions would slip from mind and like last year's foliage disappear into humus. When Vicki's mother learned that Vicki planned to accompany me to Houston, she ordered Vicki not to go. "What's this Uncle Claridge to you?" she shouted. "He's never done anything for Sam and hasn't any money. While Sam is in Texas, you come to Princeton and clean my house."

School ended in May, and in June, the children went to camp in Maine. Time passed, and I could not delay the trip. On July 11, Vicki and I set off for Houston, 1,817 miles away. I told Vicki that I wanted to drive because "driving was American." "Yes," Vicki answered, "this will be a voyage of personal discovery." I also drove because if we had flown, I would have been forced to rent a car in Texas. I am not comfortable in rented cars. I worry that I will have a wreck, the insurance won't cover the collision, and I will end, as my grandfather always predicted for himself, "in the poorhouse."

We stopped the first time at 11:15 in the morning in Duchess County, New York, one hundred and three miles and two hours and six minutes from home. Traveling made us hungry, and we munched apples. "I'm going to have to high-jack a Frito-Lay truck," Vicki said, finishing her apple. Chicory and Queen Anne's lace blossomed on the shoulder of the road, and I picked a buttonhole for Vicki. I noticed flowers throughout the trip. Wildflowers had been planted in the median along Highway 81 in Virginia. Early in July cosmos and narrow-leaved sunflower bloomed, the colors not bright enough, however, to distract vision from billboards advertising Hardee's, Texaco, Day's Inn, Econo-Lodge, Sunoco, and Long John Silver's. "A Certified Business Location," signs declared at county lines. Perched atop poles thin as the legs of wading birds, signs hovered over the highway, appearing eager to snap up the remnants of Virginia's natural beauty. Years ago, when I crossed the border of Virginia headed for Richmond or Nashville, my heart leaped up, pounding at the thought of being in the South. On the trip to Houston I felt no emotion. Virginia seemed an anonymous business location with no soul, or history.

The trip to Texas took three and a half days, and the landscape passed like sleepers under rails. Occasionally a sleeper bulged out of the right of way, jarring me into observation: in southern Pennsylvania, fat silos and barns at the edges of soft fields; below the Shenandoah Valley, galleries of kudzu sculpture; cedar trees in Tennessee; and in Alabama, religious slogans sprayed on bridge abutments, "Trust Jesus" and "Are You Ready for the

Lord?" Beside the Boy Scout Headquarters in Birmingham loomed the warning "Don't Be Caught Dead Without Jesus." Vicki labeled Highway 59 slicing across Mississippi "the road of endless pines." Shutters of pines blocked vision, hiding, we speculated, ravages of lumbering. Tumbled along the shoulders of the road, dead armadillos dried into silver gourds. Driving across Louisiana on Highways 10 and 12 was nightmarish. Trains of trucks buckled toward Texas, tires thumping, shattering in potholes, leaving slabs of rubber thick on the road.

Vicki and I spent nights in motels built in strips outside small towns: Harrisonburg, Virginia; Tuscaloosa, Alabama; Sulphur, Louisiana; and then on the way home, Lebanon, Tennessee, and Christiansburg, Virginia. From our room in the Shoney's Inn in Harrisonburg, I watched the moon rise over a Food Lion grocery store. Parked along the road in front of the store was a tractor trailer, loaded with Eukanuba dog food. Driving tired me, and at motels, I talked only to desk clerks. Still, when checking out of the Shoney's Inn in Tuscaloosa, I noticed a newspaper on the counter. The lead article discussed the introduction of prayer into public school. "Oh, no," I muttered, looking at the paper, "not prayer again." "Why shouldn't there be religion in schools?" said a woman standing behind me. "In my town," I explained wearily, "students come from many countries. They speak twenty-six languages and probably belong to fifteen different faiths. Schools would have to chop reading and mathematics from the curriculum if teachers said prayers appropriate to all the religions." "No," the woman said briskly. "There is only one God. Teachers only need to say one prayer."

On the road dinners and breakfasts were ordinary. Most mornings we ate in Waffle Houses, ordering coffee and pecan waffles. At night we were weary and ate in restaurants close to motels. Lunches were better. Often I drove some distance off the interstate searching for places to eat. In Jackson, Tennessee, we ate at Logan's Roadhouse, "Named One of the Country's Top Ten Steakhouses," a red banner proclaimed. A wash of peanut shells rumpled across the floor of Logan's. When we sat down, a waiter brought us a tin bucket brimming with unshelled peanuts. I snatched a handful, then ordered iced tea and a steak. On the third day I stopped at the Welcome Center on Route 12 in Louisiana, just across the border from Mississippi. I asked the woman behind the counter to suggest a good restaurant. "I can't do that," she said. "There are many restaurants along the road, and I am not allowed to recommend one." "But," she continued, staring hard at me, "why don't you drive thirty minutes down the highway? When you come to Covington, take Route 190 north. About two miles up the road on the right, you will see a restaurant named Licata's. Although regulations forbid me to recommend any eating establishment, I think you will find Licata's satisfactory."

Our routine was simple. Every evening Vicki bought postcards. After dinner she wrote her parents in New Jersey and the children in Maine. While she wrote, I watched movies on television. I always fell asleep before the films ended. I did most of the driving, and while I drove, Vicki dozed. To pass time I played the radio. Usually I listened to classical music. At the beginning of the trip I sampled country music. Alas, the lyrics of country music have been "dumbed down." A jukebox of songs celebrated ignoramuses who owned pickup trucks. Passing miles in the company of illiterates who didn't know the proper use of *lie* and *lay* did not appeal to me. In contrast I enjoyed listening to preachers. Rarely, though, did I hear a complete sermon. Stations that broadcast sermons rarely had enough power to jump from one valley to another. Once I heard a man mention "secondary virginity." Unfortunately, at that moment I drove over a ridge and missed the definition of the phrase. Much that preachers said puzzled me. "The law of nature is to do the thing," one man declared, "and with the thing you'll have the power." Occasionally I joined a congregation in responding, saying, "now you're preaching" or "tell it, brother, tell it." One time after the spirit moved me, Vicki raised her left eyelid, shook her head, and said, "Jesus." "Amen," I added. I especially enjoyed gospel jubilees, almost all of which were sponsored by funeral homes. Of course, funeral homes cannot decorously underwrite many programs. An exercise class, for example, would be inappropriate. Most people who patronize funeral homes will lose flesh without subjecting their remains to regimens of diet or exercise. Moreover, I doubt many funeral homes sponsor dating services on the radio. "SFNVDIPC," or, single female not very decayed in perpetual care, "seeks well-preserved grave male for out of body experience. Necrophiliacs need not apply. 'You can take it with you.'"

In Houston I found a nursing home for Uncle Coleman and straightened out his affairs. Feeling satisfied, I drove home slowly. We dallied for an afternoon in Hershey, Pennsylvania, exploring Hershey's Chocolate World and hunting presents for the children. Earrings shaped like candy kisses and wrapped in silver, green, red, and gold paper cost $4.95 a pair. A mouse pad decorated with sketches of Reese's Peanut Butter Cups cost $8.50. I considered buying a piñata shaped like a giant kiss, but an empty piñata cost $14.95. Eventually we bought each of the children tin boxes. Five and a half inches tall and costing $5.95 apiece, the boxes sat on bases four inches square. Depicted on each box was a candy store dating from the 1920s. While a little girl in a straw hat munched a candy bar, a woman behind a counter wrapped a carton in pink paper. "A Meal in Itself," declared the caption under the illustration. In Storrs Vicki crammed kisses into the boxes, buying the candy at CVS, where prices were cheaper than in Pennsylvania.

I drove back through Arkansas in order to pass through middle Tennessee. Mother and Father, Grandma and Grandpa, and Great-grandfather Pickering and his wife Eliza, my daughter's namesake, are buried in Carthage. Born in Ohio, Great-grandfather had been a Union soldier in the Civil War. Later, he was postmaster of Carthage. Carved on the stone above his grave in the old town cemetery was "A Zealous Christian. A Gallant Soldier. A Faithful Official. A Friend to Man." After his first wife died, Great-grandfather married Etta Haynie, known to family as Cousin Etta. Several of Cousin Etta's children died young. Great-grandfather himself smothered one child, rolling over her while asleep in bed. Beside Great-grandfather's marker stood a small stone with a lamb carved on top. Time had worn the lamb to a white lump, and the child's name had vanished. Although lichens splattered the stone, the inscription was still legible. I lay on the grave, and tracing letters with my fingers puzzled out the words: "God needed one more angel child / Amid his shining band. / And He bent with longing smile / And clasped our baby's hand."

Pickerings lived in Carthage for a century. Great-grandfather helped establish the Sunday school in the Methodist church, and his name appeared on a stained-glass window. For his part Grandfather had been the first editor, Coleman said, of the *Carthage Courier*, the town's weekly newspaper. Recollection of a family rarely endures beyond a generation. My grandmother died in 1963, and no one I talked to in Carthage had heard the name Pickering. When I mentioned the old graveyard, a woman said, "I have lived in Carthage most of my life, but I didn't know white people were buried there." Carthaginians are not great readers. There is no bookstore in the town, and the Smith County Library occupies a small building behind the courthouse. In my essays I describe a fictional Carthage, and I wondered how many of my books the library owned. The answer was one. "Books," Vicki said, "are the scat that people who write leave behind as they travel the path of life. It's not reasonable to think your droppings will interest strangers." What one person thinks a dropping, another believes treasure. I am forever drawn buzzing to the petals of history. Outside the Smith County Courthouse stood a war memorial. I counted names on the memorial. One hundred and forty Smith Countians died fighting for the South in the Civil War, among them Robert and Hugh McClarin, brothers or cousins of my great-grandmother.

At a florist store I bought flowers for the graves of Mother and Father, Grandma and Grandpa, in the Mountain Cemetery. The arrangement was crisp with baby's breath, pink carnations, and white and yellow daisies. "The flowers won't last in this heat," Vicki said. "I don't want them to live long," I answered. A sugar maple stood at the foot of the family plot. When Grandfather died in 1952, Grandmother had a stone bench placed under the tree. Often she drove to the graveyard and, sitting on the bench, pondered the past. I had not visited the graveyard since Father's death in 1990. Someone had shifted the bench. Instead of facing Pickerings, the bench looked toward the Gores. "Shouldn't you tell the caretaker to move the bench back," Vicki said. "No," I said, "Pickerings are forgotten, but there are still Gores spry enough to sit and ruminate." Recollection is fragile and often depends upon association. I tried to buy postcards of Carthage, hoping that pictures would bring place and story to mind. No store sold postcards depicting Carthage. "There aren't any postcards of the town," a man said. "Not even of the courthouse?" I asked. "No," he said, "anyway the courthouse is being renovated. Maybe when the remodeling is over, we'll have cards."

For years fictional characters in my books have misbehaved in Red Boiling Springs, a small town in Macon County twenty-three miles north of Carthage near the Kentucky border. Early in the century Red Boiling Springs was a thriving resort. In summer vacationers crowded streets, living in hotels and boarding houses and drinking mineral waters, these last named white, red, black, double and twist, and free stone. Despite my writing I had never visited Macon County, and when I learned in Carthage that three hotels had been refurbished, I drove to Red Boiling Springs. The road curved around granite hills like aluminum around muffins in a baking pan. Small creeks wound through coves. On bottomlands above the bends of creeks tobacco grew leafy and green. Corn spread down valleys that opened slowly like fingers being pried apart. "If you promised not to listen to any preachers," Vicki said, "I would live here."

Vicki and I stayed at the old Cloyd Hotel, renamed the Thomas House. Dinner and breakfast and a large room cost seventy dollars. The original Cloyd had been wood. When the building burned at the beginning of the century, the hotel was rebuilt using bricks molded and fired on the grounds. The Thomas House sat atop a knobby hill. About the hotel grew a collar of white oaks, tulip trees, sugar maples, and shagbark hickories. In the evening a hutch of rabbits appeared under the trees, and quail called from a pasture. A storm blew the nest of a robin out of a maple, and while I sat in a rocking chair waiting for dinner, a fledgling perched atop the back of a white wicker chair.

In cleaning Coleman's house I strained my back. Rarely do I linger onshore, pushing my toes hesitatingly through experience. On learning that I could bathe in mineral waters, then have a massage at Armour's Hotel, I plunged in kicking. Earlier in the day I stopped at a well and, sharing a jug with an old man, drank two pints of red water, the liquid being, I was told, a diuretic. The man said that several years earlier he lost his house in "the great flood." Nevertheless he continued to drink mineral water, water being, as he put it, "part of my life, good and bad." While bathing I did not sip the black water, and the heat made my back feel good. Even better was the massage, at least until I got up. When I stood, pain slashed across my back and stabbed down my right leg. Taking small, neat steps, I returned to the Thomas House and changed clothes for dinner. Consisting of country ham and platters of vegetables, white beans, turnip greens, tomatoes, and spring onions, dinner was served in an ornate Victorian hall. As I shuffled into the hall, my back cracked like a shack swept off its foundation by high water, and I wondered if I could sit through the meal.

Although the middle-aged male sometimes thinks so, man is not back alone. Halfway through the meal, something I ate on the road pitched up from my stomach and despite the waterspout of pain spraying up my back, I rushed outside and vomited next to a large tulip tree, a buck rabbit eyeing me warily. I did not return to the dining hall. Instead I pulled myself upstairs to my room and, putting on pajamas, fell into bed. While Vicki swam smoothly through rich dish after rich dish, I tried to float motionless on the mattress. On the table next to me lay a guest book signed by previous occupants of the room. To pass time I read their comments. "Like a taste of honey" a woman wrote, adding, "my friend and I had a wonderful night swim, and we saw four sweet little frogs." "People who turn back time by loving an old building build the future," declared a man from Illinois; "the beauty and tranquillity of this place will always be with us." By the time Vicki returned to the room, I had a high fever. Because I could no longer see words, Vicki read to me. "Our first real honeymoon in thirteen years of marriage. This was the perfect place," she read, before adding the personal note, "not for us." Next she read stories from the December 1993 issue of *Dog Fancy,* a magazine she plucked from a rack in the bathroom. I remember only one story, an account of a German shepherd hit by a train in northern Indiana. For a week the dog lay in bushes near the roadbed. Then a conductor on the South Shore Railway rescued him. Although in terrible shape, the dog survived. My own survival seemed doubtful, and before falling asleep I instructed Vicki to bury me in Carthage if I died in Tennessee. I also own a space in Hollywood Cemetery in Richmond, and I told Vicki that if I lingered until we reached Virginia, she could bury me in Richmond.

My sleep was short. Instead of dead, my stomach was alive. Several times during the night I crawled into the bathroom, my back making walking too painful. Once in the bathroom I crouched on all fours and hung my head over the toilet, resembling, Vicki said, "a turtle creeping across a highway." The next morning I felt well enough to drive but not to eat. The road, I told Vicki, would divert my attention from my stomach. I was wrong. A dozen miles east of Carthage, I pulled into a rest area. While Vicki bought a Coca-Cola, I tottered down to the Caney Fork River and threw up beside yellow touch-me-not. Forty-five minutes later, east of Cookeville, I threw up again, this time into a mound of Virginia creeper. When I returned to the car, Vicki was listening to a preacher on the radio. "Jesus loves you," the man shouted. "Even poor you, sick with sin," Vicki added, looking at me.

The most unsettling part of my summer vacation, however, was not spent in Tennessee but in Texas. A clerk in an Exxon station called Houston "Los Angeles south." Superhighways bored through the city in broad channels, traffic washing through them then spilling over shoulders and down side streets in great spinning snags. At intersections lanes rose and turned over each other, the bridges first resembling aqueducts then concrete webs in which I felt stuck, unable to shake loose, traffic jams trussing me tighter than silk . Coleman lived near Memorial Park in central Houston. Known as the Loop, Highway 610 circled the area, turning the center of the city into a drain, commuters swirling into it in the morning, then spewing out in the evening. Clambering onto the lip of the drain was frightening. Cars swept along in wild currents, the automobiles behind me always racing forward as if they were intent upon washing over me, bumper and trunk. Every day I drove the Loop. "Dante got things wrong," Vicki said; "the circles of Hell are cities surrounded by highways." Only once, though, did a driver honk at me. He was from Connecticut, the only Connecticut license I saw south of Pennsylvania, and he waved, stuck his right thumb up, and smiled. "Mexicans are the dangerous drivers," Coleman's yard man said; "they think they are riding burros. When they get flustered, they take their hands off the wheel. Once you let go of the reins, a car doesn't trot to the side of a trail to munch cactus. A car bucks and kills."

Vicki and I spent much time in Houston driving. We bought groceries and household cleansers at Randall's supermarket on the corner of Shepherd and Westheimer. We took Coleman's clothes to the laundry, then bought him new underwear, trousers, shirts, pajamas, socks, and a bathrobe at Sears. At Target I purchased a clothes hamper. At Radio Shack I bought a telephone and at Circuit City a color television with a twenty-inch screen. Coleman refused to leave his house, but Vicki and I ate lunches and dinners in restaurants, in part to raise our spirits. A constellation of chores whorled about, wearing us down. When we tried to solve one problem, another blinked and distracted us. We stayed in Amanda's room. Temperature in Houston was in the 90s, and humidity was so high that water rolled down our faces. The air conditioner in Coleman's house was broken, and globs of thick paint sealed all the windows. After I found a putty knife in the garage, Vicki and I spent the first afternoon in Houston digging paint away from windows. We slept in a three-quarters bed. The left side of the mattress was higher than the right, and the bed sloped sharply, tumbling Vicki against me no matter her efforts to grope upward.

Sleeping was so difficult that we stayed up late every night, cleaning the house. For years closets had served Coleman as dumpsters. A landfill of paper covered the pantry floor. Through the trash roaches had beaten paths resembling trails worn by voles under high grass. For the last thirty years neither Amanda nor Coleman had thrown away correspondence, and when I opened drawers of desks and chests, papers exploded upward. From Coleman's room alone Vicki and I removed twenty-six Hefty garbage bags of printed matter, most solicitations from conservative churches and political groups. "He gave all his money to them," the yard man said. "I tried to stop him, but the letters kept coming. When he quit donating money, they telephoned and pressured him to send more. They even came to the house."

Coleman's affairs resembled a sponge, absorbing attention and energy. Not only did they dominate the present but they lowered over the future. Who was this person, I wondered, for whom I was suddenly responsible? As I cleaned house, I looked for traces of the man. On a shelf I found a postcard sent to Mrs. Douglas Wikle in Franklin, Tennessee, in May 1912. Printed on the back of the card was "the other Pickering boy—Coleman Enoch—at 1 year 6 months old." On the front of the card was a picture of Coleman. He sat on the lip of a bench. He wore a white sweater with big buttons, a small stocking cap high on his forehead, a white shift, woolen leggings, and patent leather slippers. Resembling the faded ink on the card, Coleman's expression was tentative. His mouth turned down at the corners, and his eyes seemed disturbed. His head tilted to the left, and he appeared on the verge of crying.

Beneath a stack of books in the living room lay *The Commo-*

dore, the yearbook of Vanderbilt University. Coleman, I discovered, was vice president of the class of 1931. During the Second World War Coleman served in the Army. In a cardboard box in the garage I found his "Separation Qualification Record." Coleman entered the Army on February 12, 1943, and served in the Quartermaster Corps, being discharged as a Captain on August 8, 1946. Typed on the bottom of the Record was an account of his responsibilities. "Commanded the 1686th labor Supervision Company in France," the Record stated. "Was responsible for supervision of a stockade enclosing prisoners of war, and directed the operation of an army bakery. Was in complete charge of all administrative and operational activities of unit, having less than 100 troops and approximately 2,000 prisoners of war. Served in one major campaign in European Theatre of Operations."

Under the Record lay a letter sent to Coleman from Bremen on March 15, 1946. A former prisoner of war named Oscar wrote the letter. "It is a long time ago since I left the storage # 2," Oscar recounted, "and couldn't write a few words to you. Now I am discharged and I am free. It took us about 5 weeks to get home and we had lots of trouble. The Prisoner Office didn't know anything about our discharging and so they send us to the French, but thanks God the American Chaplain saved us all." In Bremen Oscar applied for a job in a military bakery. "I showed your letter to the commanding officer," Oscar recounted, "and he said to me 1st Lt. Pickering is a friend of myn and was very glad to hear about you. And I got a job right away. But the only trouble is that the German Labor Office does'nt give me the permission to live here in Bremen. So I ask you kindly Lt. Sir to write to 1st Lt. Ray V. Brown commanding officer of the QM Class I Bakery 4428 QM Service Camp APO 751. May be he can help to get the permission and to get a room for me. I hope Lt. Sir you will try to do the best an I thank you lots for it. I was for ever your old Oscar."

Hanging behind the door of a closet was Coleman's army jacket. Moths had gorged on the wool, and the jacket looked too small for Eliza. As presents for Edward I removed two brass ornaments from the lapels of the jacket. On the ornaments appeared the insignia of the Quartermaster Corps, a gold eagle stretching its wings over a blue wheel. A sword and a key crossed the wheel in diameters and formed an X in the center. I found only one other momento from the war in the house. While stationed in Britain, Coleman traveled to Yorkshire and visited the town of Pickering. A token from that trip served as a bookmark in a copy of Tennyson's poems. The bookmark lay at the beginning of Tennyson's "The Two Voices," the first stanza of which stated, "A still small voice spake unto me, / 'Thou art so full of mystery, / Were it not better not to be?'" The bookmark itself was a business card, one and a half by three inches. Printed in the center of the card was PICKERINGS GARAGE. In the upper left corner of the card was the garage's telephone number, "34"; in the lower left, the address, "Eastgate. Pickering. Yorks." The owner of the garage signed the card, writing "Ronald Wm. Pickering" across the top.

Practically every drawer in Coleman's house contained business cards. The only other card that interested me, however, advertised Binkley's Service Station at 61 Hermitage Avenue in Nashville. Printed on the back of the card was "Sing While You Drive," cautionary instruction for vehicular harmony. "At 45 miles per hour," the card urged, "sing—'Highways Are Happy Ways.' At 55 miles, sing—'I'm But a Stranger Here, Heaven Is My Home.' At 65 miles, sing—'Nearer, My God, To Thee!' At 75 miles, sing—'When the Roll Is Called Up Yonder, I'll Be There.' At 85 miles, sing—'Lord, I'm Coming Home.'"

The little boy perched uneasily on the bench grew into a tentative man, a person who changed jobs often and whose mother lectured him until her death. In the drawer of Coleman's bedside table I found fifty-six letters written by Grandma Pickering. Grandma wrote the letters in 1962–63, the last year of her life, when she was eighty-two years old. Most letters were six or eight pages long, but several consisted of sixteen pages. Grandma rarely commented on worldly doings, although in one letter she said John Kennedy's eyes looked "reptilely." Usually she wrote about family or happenings in Carthage. When an acquaintance died, she mentioned the man's retarded son, "12 or 13 years old. It is a sad affair. His mind runs to calling girls on the 'phone and sometimes his language is questionable." Occasionally she visited the graveyard. Once she put a red geranium on Grandpa's grave. "He liked geraniums," she recounted, adding that he "loved to smell the leaves." On another occasion she placed hydrangeas on the grave. "Your daddy," she wrote, "loved flowers and I want to carry them up there. Maybe he can see me and the flowers."

Coleman was a poor correspondent, and if my father's complaints were accurate, a neglectful son. Far from Coleman, Grandma pasted imaginary shared experiences across pages. "Did you see Groucho Marx last night?" she asked. "I look at it, for I think that you probably will be seeing it, too." "I do wish I could see you today," she said. "Did you see the golf games on T.V. played in Chicago? While I know very little about golf, I saw it as I thought maybe you were looking at it." Despite the wistful strain in the letters, Grandma was not melancholy. Only once did she mention being out of sorts, and then she did not linger on mood, sensibly attributing her feelings to the weather. "This is a dreary day in Tennessee," she wrote; "maybe it has something to do with my spirits, for I seem to be in a dark mood."

In a storage room I found a picture taken when Grandma was young. Three strings of pearls circled her neck, then slipped down her bosom. Above her forehead a mass of brown hair rose like a meadow, waving and spilling in an autumn breeze. Her lips were full but clamped together. Unlike Coleman's eyes flickering on the edge of change, her eyes were locked into the impression she wanted to create: a confident and capable adult. Perhaps Grandma's strength drove Coleman to Texas. Advice peppered her letters, not the sort of thing to endear a mother to a fifty-two-year-old son, much less to an impressionable boy. After urging Coleman to buy a new suit, preferably "a light worsted which will be useful the year round," she wrote, "you must have cuff-link shirts and they must extend beyond the coat sleeve. You see I notice what the well-dressed man is wearing. And you need a hat. A man should wear a hat to be well-dressed." She concluded, saying, "I would love to be there to go with you when you select your suit." In another letter she told him to make sure all his suits fit well. Fashions, she noted, had changed. Trousers were shorter and snugger than in the past. Coats, she explained, "are not as full in the back, and sleeves should show the shirt cuff when the arm is extended."

Grandma lectured Coleman on work habits. She urged him to get to the office early and finish tasks before leaving at the end of the day. "Never be late at your work, Coleman," she wrote; "this is one of the most important items in every business. *So listen to me.* It will pay off." Grandma harped on order and public appearance. "Son," she said, "*be sure* and keep your desk in good order. Every thing counts in business. *Be* careful to see that your desk is always in good order and appearance." Coleman's buying a Ford Comet provided the occasion for a lecture on car care. "Write me about your insurance now," she advised him. "Drop into a place and have the car cleaned. Keep it nice. Don't load it up with litter. Put a carton in it to hold *extras.* This carton could be kept inside on the back floor for convenience."

At one time Coleman borrowed money. Grandma sent him a check and advice. "Coleman," she preached, "please don't go into debt ever again—you make enough to save some of it, so *please* don't go into debt. The time will surely come when savings will come in for some thing worth while. Be sure and have an individual bank account. There is no other satisfactory arrangement and will be better for both you and Amanda. Your daddy and I always had individual bank accounts. This arrangement does not interfere with either of you issuing checks to the other when needed. *And Stop Borrowing.*" Time changed little. Coleman's affairs were still muddled, and I had become Grandma. Occasionally I thought only the Great First Cause could establish order and put an end, as Vicki put it, "to the reign of chaos and old age."

When Coleman left Tennessee, he, in effect, broke from family. Only rarely did he write Father. "I *do* wish you would write him," Grandma wrote, speaking of Father. "It hurts him that you seemingly don't care to write him. And he has always loved you so much and really wants news of you. He asked me Sunday, as he always does, if I had heard from you." When close relatives died, Coleman neglected to write the survivors. When a relative married, he forgot to send a present. "Have you ever written Sammy a thank you for your gifts on Christmas?" Grandma asked, speaking of me. "Please do that. Your *gifts* were reminders that he was thinking of you and loved you. It is an unpardonable lapse of decent courtesy to ignore a kindness and among friends often strains a deep and long lasting relationship. Somehow, I just can't let my appreciation go unexpressed." Coleman was not always so slack as Grandma's letters implied. For Christmas in 1961, he sent me a clothes brush and a shoe shine kit. Among letters in Coleman's bedroom I found a thank-you note I sent from Sewanee. I had, I said, made fraternity pledges use the kit several times on my shoes, adding, "they are good slave labor."

I read Grandma's letters not only because I wondered about Coleman's character but also because I was curious about myself. Amid the letters lurked glimpses of me and hints of traits shared with Grandma or Coleman. Instead of the occasional hazy sighting, however, I discovered snapshots, all focused and clear despite being viewed through the long shutter of years. In my essays I wander days and fields, sniffing flowers and sauntering through hours. One of Grandma's letters described what became my literary method. "When he comes up here," she wrote, recalling one of my visits to Carthage, "he goes through my books, even up stairs, and brings out pictures and letters. He just lives to prowl." I resemble Grandma more than Coleman. Although I often depict myself as relaxed, I am hardworking and intense, *"very tenacious,"* Grandma said. When a dean at Sewanee flattered Father by saying I was one of four leaders in the college, Grandma wrote, "I told Samuel not to mention it to Sammy as he will try to lead the four." As Grandma's letters accurately described my character so did a letter Vicki wrote Coleman and Amanda from Latakia, Syria, in February 1980. Vicki and I had been married seven months. "I could not be happier in my marriage," she wrote; "I am convinced I have the most wonderful husband on earth." I wanted to show the letter to Vicki and tell her that I thought I had the most wonderful wife on earth. Sixteen years, though, changes the way husbands and wives talk to and about each other, and I did nothing, halting on the borderland, as the old gospel song puts it, in my diffidence behaving more like Coleman than Grandma.

While cleaning the house, I found letters written by Father. Unlike Coleman, Father was decisive. Grandpa Pickering died from prostate cancer in 1952. The cancer was diagnosed in 1947. On February 7, 1947, Father wrote Coleman about the illness. "I have been faced," he wrote, "with an almost unanswerable problem and have done what I consider best. I hope you will agree. Dr. Gayden told me that there was a low grade malignancy which wasn't too much of a surprise as I suspected it from the way he acted. So did mother. However, I did not tell her. Knowing her temperament, it would only give her something else to worry about and she would let daddy know immediately, either directly or unintentionally." Father described the progress of the disease, noting that the doctor "said daddy could live for say 3 years, which of course knocked me. It goes without saying it could be less." I felt close to Father when I read the letter. As he assumed responsibility for Grandpa and decided not to tell his parents about the disease, so I assumed responsibility for Coleman, acting in ways that others might criticize but that I thought right. In the pantry I found another letter from Father, this one written in 1983, after he and Mother visited Vicki and me in Connecticut. Father was in good spirits, and the tone of letter resembled that of my essays. Edward was five months old. "Edward," Father said, "seems to have a different build from Francis. As Sammy says, 'Francis has the Pickering shanks.'" "Looks like a lot of my friends, mostly male," Father wrote later in the letter, "are handing in their dinner pails—to paraphrase P. G. Wodehouse."

In Houston I realized that I would spend more time caring for Coleman, a stranger, than I had caring for Father. I suspected that Coleman would become so much a part of my present that he would push Father out of mind. Consequently I scoured Coleman's house for traces of Father. In a copy of *The Early Poems of Henry Wadsworth Longfellow,* published in Boston in 1886, I found an eight-and-a-half-by-eleven-inch sheet of paper. The paper had been folded into quarters. Printed on one side was the reading list for a course in English history that Father took at Vanderbilt. In the margin beside the list Father doodled, writing the last letters of the alphabet, *p* through *z,* then playing four games of tic-tac-toe. On another quarter of the paper appeared notes jotted down during a lecture on Laurence Sterne's novel *Tristram Shandy.* I recognized the novel because Father wrote "Uncle Toby," the name of one of the main characters in the book. Sterne's novel was bawdy, and although the notes were impressionistic, they smacked of moral criticism. "Whim, jumbled, striking and informal style," Father scribbled, before adding, "coarse features—his age, however, oddity, dullness, indecency."

I brought *The Early Poems* back to Connecticut. When Coleman's affairs weighed me down, I read them. The poetry was simple, and the verse flowed so cleanly that the poems reassured me, unlike the jumbled course of life itself. "Under a spreading chestnut-tree / The village smithy stands; / The smith, a mighty man is he, / With large and sinewy hands; / And the muscles of his brawny arms / Are strong as iron bands." From Texas I brought another book to Connecticut, *Proceedings of the Grand Chapter of the Order of the Eastern Star, State of Tennessee 1964.* During 1927–28, Grandma served as Worthy Grand Matron for Tennessee, and the *Proceedings* contained a memorial to her. "She was a friend," a poem began, "whose heart was good, / Who walked with folks and understood." Although the tribute was generous, I kept the *Proceedings* because the book contained lists of names. Villages of country folk people my essays. Naming characters is difficult, and amid the *Proceedings,* names seemed to be waiting for me, if not "on that peaceful shore," at least along the margins of pages. A choir of sweet gospel singers appeared in the *Proceedings*: Barsha, Geneva, Rubye, Novileen, Argell, Ilo, Electa, Leola, Evadine, Minnie, and Inelle.

In "A Psalm of Life," Longfellow said that some people left footprints on the sands of time. Sight of the prints, Longfellow declared, invigorated the forlorn and the shipwrecked. Amid the shoals of paper and the sandy banks of bureaucracy surrounding Coleman's life, I was occasionally forlorn. Never, however, was I shipwrecked. I sorted through matters like a mariner sounding shallows with a hand lead. Although the work was tiring, fragments of the past bucked me up, glimpses of relatives, not Longfellow's vision of footprints, but indentations of heels here and there. At the beginning of the Civil War, Great-grandfather joined the Ohio Volunteer Infantry. In 1863, when he was nineteen years old, he became adjutant of the 1st Cavalry Regiment of the Middle Tennessee Volunteers. One night I found a packet of his papers, including his "Muster-In Roll." On June 9, in Carthage, he entered the regiment as 1st Lieutenant. W. B. Stokes, colonel of the regiment, signed the Roll. Great-grandfather signed up for a term of "three years or during the war." He did not bring a horse or "horse equiptments" with him when he joined the regiment. After the war Great-grandfather settled in Carthage. Among the papers in the packet was a bill of sale for land bought in Carthage in 1873. The land cost $2,800 and was five acres "more or less."

In 1881 Great-grandfather was chief clerk of the Tennessee House of Representatives. At the end of the session he applied "To the Honorable Secretary of War" for "a place as Investigating Agent of the Quartermasters Department." Accompanying the application was a petition signed by all members of the House "present at the session, those not signing being absent on account of sickness." Great-grandfather wrote the petition. He was known for his penmanship, and script flowed over the page like a garden across a lawn. Thick stems of letters swept upward into airy blossoms. Words stretched in lines like yew hedges. Capitals rose in the middle of pages, resembling bronze statues in lily ponds: Athena, a helmet pushed high on her forehead, or Hercules, a knobby club hanging from his right hand and, draped over his shoulders, the skin of the Nemean Lion. Ink on the petition had faded, turning red and Georgian. From a distance words appeared bricks, the margins of the pages stone dressing atop walls. Great-grandfather's signature loomed at the bottoms of pages like pavilions at the end of gravel walks, the letters of his initials *W, B,* and *P* ornamental urns, the other letters latticework.

The contents of Coleman's house were gothic, not neoclassical, Great-grandfather's penmanship just one gargoyle among many. On a shelf above the packet sat a small wire crown, six and a half inches in diameter, seven triangles rising to sharp points above a wreath. Circling the crown was a string of plastic pearls. Lining the inside of the crown was a strip of blue plastic. Stamped on the plastic in white letters was "WITH LOVE FROM YOUR FOURTH GRADE—1968–1969—TO OUR QUEEN OF A TEACHER—MRS. PICKERING." "There is a Reaper," Longfellow wrote, "whose name is Death, / And, with his sickle keen, / He reaps the bearded grain at a breath, / And the flowers that grow between." Amanda taught for forty years. For the last thirty years of her career she kept all school correspondence, cramming letters from students and notes from parents into dressers. When papers bounded out of drawers like clowns clambering through the windows and doors of small cars at circuses, she packed her correspondence in cardboard boxes and stored them under beds. In cleaning house, I resembled the Reaper, throwing away not simply paper but Amanda's life.

Some flowers avoided my sickle, bending like the stems of dandelions at night, then rising into notice during the day. Before school started each fall, Amanda wrote her last class. "Now that vacation ends and we must think of school again," she wrote. "I think once more of our little class of last year. To you, as a member of that group, I want to express my sincere appreciation for your kindness and thoughtfulness toward me as we worked together. As you continue through life, I shall derive much pleasure in feeling that I have contributed in part to each achievement of yours. That is a teacher's reward." At Amanda's retirement in 1973, friends sang "Ode to Amanda," a song written by a fellow teacher and sung to the tune of "Tennessee Waltz." "We are toasting to a darling," the song began, "with that Tennessee schmaltz."

Stuck to the bottom of a box was a three-by-five-inch note card. "Poor Amanda," I thought after reading the card. "Dear Mrs. Pickering," a parent wrote, "I am grateful for Marcia's Arithmetic grade. She was very pleased when she was able to stay with you after school, and it seemed to do wonders for her. I hope that you will be able to help her more this next six weeks after school. I am indeed grateful to you for your every effort." In a desk I found issues of *The Raven,* a newspaper compiled by students at Poe Elementary School. "Our pet turtle which Chris Calloway brought to our room has escaped from his home on the Science table. If anyone sees a stray turtle please return him to Classroom 2," a correspondent wrote from Amanda's third grade in 1947. Perhaps because the climate is warmer, schoolroom turtles are more active in Texas than in Connecticut. In 1949 Snappy escaped from Amanda's classroom. "He was tame," the reporter recounted, "but one day decided to leave. We think he became jealous of our other pets and decided to climb out the window. We hope he has found a winter home under the building." Amanda's room resembled a zoo, quick with butterflies, grasshoppers, goldfish, ants, caterpillars, frogs, and a snake. The doings of these creatures were exciting, and the children did not mourn Snappy's loss. "One of our happiest moments," the reporter noted at the end of his article, "came when we discovered six baby snails in our bowl of thirteen tropical fish. The mother snail now has plenty of company and helpers to keep the aquarium clean."

In 1963, a member of the "Editorial Staff" contributed a poem entitled "Secret Garden" to *The Poe Tribune*. "There is a secret garden," the poem began, "I do not know just where, / Beautiful roses and snowdrops, / Climbing up the wall." While cleaning Coleman's house, I imagined discovering a secret garden, one bright, Vicki said, "with thousand dollar bills." Instead, I found weeds, not green and blooming but woody tissue, gray and brown, the dress of widowed nature. Still, amid broken stems and tattered rosettes of basal leaves lurked hints of forgotten springs and compost rich enough to nourish my prowling interest. In a drawer lay a page torn from a Nashville telephone directory. Three-fifths of the way down the third column on the page, I read CY2-3515, the number for the telephone at Mother and Father's house at 4402 Iroquois Avenue, the CY standing, I recalled, for Cypress.

In a green tin box that once contained Edgeworth Pipe Tobacco, the "High Grade Sliced" variety manufactured by "Larus and Bro." in Richmond, I found the badge of the United Daughters of the Confederacy. Shaped like a cross, the badge was cut from a piece of metal one and five-sixteenths inches square. Stamped in the center of the cross was a Confederate flag. On the other side of the cross a wreath surrounded the words "DEO VINDICE" and the dates of the Civil War, 1861–65. The box contained a miscellany of things, all, except the badge, pertaining to smoking. Under the cross was a cigarette lighter. Swelling in the middle, then tapering so that both ends curved like the bow of a ship, the lighter was smooth and streamlined. The lighter advertised "Fruehauf trailers," and a trailer stretched across one side of the lighter. Also in the box were two matchboxes, the first advertising the Ambassador Hotel in New York at Park Avenue and 51st and 52nd streets. "Enjoy the Best in New York," the matchbook urged. The Plains Hotel in Cheyenne, Wyoming, appeared on the second matchbook. "Famous for FOOD," the spine of the matchbook bragged. The hotel itself consisted of four stories of rooms, then a bottom floor containing, a black sign with white letters assured travelers, a coffee shop.

As age scrubs event from memory, so time reduces experience to fragments. Scattered throughout the house were postcards, souvenirs of trips and places that meant little to me. In a cream pitcher I found a card depicting the "New Hotel Shamrock" in Gainesboro, Tennessee, a two-story rectangular brick building resembling a high school. Two rows of blue and yellow propeller-driven planes stretched like a stately avenue through the center of a card, saying "Greetings from Elgin Fields, Florida." Over the avenue buzzed thirty-five planes. The planes were different sizes and colors and reminded me of the bees that feed on goldenrod in early fall. Sketched on nine cards were pictures of buildings at the "New York World's Fair, 1964–65," among others, the Christian Science Pavilion, the House of Better Living, the Masonic Brothers Center, and the Travelers Insurance Companies Pavilion, this last resembling a scallop shell, its hinges sprung, pulling the upper red valve away from the lower white valve. Other cards depicted less exotic buildings: the Econo-Travel Motor Hotel, located at 2890 Marlane Drive, RR#1, Grove City, Ohio; and a "Dutch Pantry Family Restaurant," its roof striped red and white like a candy cane, atop a steeple in the center of the roof, a weathervane with a rooster perched on it.

As the postcards were significant to Coleman but meant nothing to me, so some things that snagged my attention probably meant little to Coleman. Amid a folder of recipes in the kitchen was a brochure advertising Old Crow bourbon. The brochure was a cutout. A crow wearing a top hat, white spats, and a red vest, and pinching a cane under his wing, clasped a scroll in his bill. Printed inside the scroll was the Old Crow's "Collection of GREAT BOURBON DRINK RECIPES," nineteen in all, most of which were for mixtures I had not tasted but that had colorful names: Ward 8, Tom and Jerry, Sazarac, and Crowbar Cocktail. "Be a good mixer," the Old Crow urged at the end of the brochure. Not only have I aged into temperance, the thought of liquor turning my gorge into a cocktail shaker, but I no longer blend into crowds. Printed matter, I am afraid, intoxicates me more than hot toddies or milk punches. Beside the telephone in Amanda's room I found a small blotter, measuring nine-by-four-inches and distributed by United Finance and Thrift Corporation. Sketched on the blotter were the license plates of all the states in the Union. The blotter was printed in 1956, before Hawaii and Alaska became states, and for that matter before everyone had friends in Pennsylvania, before philanderers migrated in lascivious hordes to Louisiana to indulge in the delights of a "Sportsman's Paradise," and before the inhabitants of New Hampshire were converted to evangelical patriotism and demanded that drivers live free or die.

In 1956 Montana dubbed itself the "Treasure State." Instead of pieces of eight, however, I discovered the September 1871 issue of *Peterson's Ladies National Magazine* in Coleman's house. Gold and silver promise future delights; pages convey present pleasure. At night I read the magazine, beginning with advertisements. "SECRET of Perpetual Beauty, and Beautiful Art of Curling Hair, *just discovered.* Sent for *10* cents," a notice stated. "Address Prof. HARVEY, Garrettsville, Ohio." A regimen of Helmbold's Catawba Grape Pills "will give NEW BLOOD, NEW VIGOR, AND NEW LIFE," promised H. T. Helmbold, a "Practical and Analytical Chemist" with offices in New York and Philadelphia. The "Grape Juice Pill," Helmbold assured valetudinarians, "is not a patented pill, put up as those ordinarily vended, but the result of 10 years of experimenting and great care in preparation." "No Nausea: No Gripping Pains: but Mild, Pleasant and Safe in Operation," Helmbold declared. "THE PRETTIEST

WOMAN in New York society, last winter, was," an advertisement claimed, "a rough-skinned, freckled-faced lady in Dayton, O., but one year ago she used Hagan's Magnolia Balm upon her face and hands with such persistency that her complexion became her greatest attraction. It will do the same for any one. It will obliterate Sallowness, Moth-patches, Ring-marks, Sunburn, etc., give a marble-like complexion, and perpetuate the bloom of youth for years." "If Coleman had studied this magazine and had started a course of Grape Pills and Magnolia Balm," I told Vicki, "every widow in Houston would be caring for him now, and we could be spending our vacation under palm trees, brows awash in coconut milk, blue water tickling our toes."

A miscellany, *Peterson's* contained a milliner's shop of patterns and sketches of fashionable dress. Some of the dresses in the magazine resembled bolts of fabric that had slipped off shelves and unraveling tumbled to floors in knots. Other dresses resembled thick curtains designed to block out light, and nature. Many dresses appeared waterlogged and so heavy that curtain rods and collar bones sagged under their weight. Still other dresses looked like chairs, lacy with tidies. Bedecked with ribbons and falls of cloth, hats reminded me of commemorative flower arrangements. In addition to clothes *Peterson's* stocked edibles. Selections from "Our New Cook-Book" contained recipes for green corn soup, gooseberry vinegar, and mock oyster fritters. "Wash some roots of salsify, grate them, and season them with pepper and salt," the recipe for this last dish instructed. "Beat the yolks of two eggs very light, stir them into a pint of milk and enough flour to make a batter. Whisk the whites dry, and add them gradually with the salsify to the batter. Dip out a spoonful at a time, and fry them like fritters."

Peterson's also contained courses of literary matters, serving poems throughout the issue almost as sorbets, then topping off the intellectual fare with a column and a half of short book reviews, resembling decorative tidbits. *Her Lord and Master* was, a reviewer declared, "a new novel by Miss Marryat, now Mrs. Rosy Church, who without being equal to George Eliot, or even Miss Mullock, is still an agreeable story-teller." Among the sweets dished out was a song entitled "O Ye Tears!" "O ye tears! O ye tears! That have long refused to flow," the song began; "Ye are welcome to my heart, thawing, thawing like the snow; / The ice-bound cloud has yielded, and the early snowdrops spring, / And the healing fountains gush, and the wilderness shall sing. / O ye tears! O ye tears!"

Composing the main literary course were short stories and excerpts from two novels, these last *The Tragedy of a Quiet Life* by Miss F. Hodgson and *The Reigning Belle* by Mrs. Ann S. Stephens. In addition to being publishers, the Petersons were booksellers, and on the back cover of the magazine an advertisement listed Stephens's complete works, each volume costing $1.50 in a "paper cover" and $1.75 in cloth. Mrs. Stephens had written sixteen novels, among them, *Married in Haste, The Old Homestead, The Wife's Secret, Fashion and Famine, The Curse of Gold,* and *Ruby Gray's Strategy.* Five short stories appeared in the magazine. Entitled "The Fatal Quarrel," the first story was an instructive tale warning readers against impetuous anger. When "just eighteen" and "freshly freed from the trammels of a boarding school," Carrie Dayton married Harry Aylmer. Almost thirty, Aylmer "was already somewhat world-worn; for, being wealthy, he had not been confined to the dull routine of a business life, but roamed the world at large, traveling in all lands, tasting every cup of pleasure." Proud and spoiled, Aylmer expected his bride to obey his commands. Initially, Carrie bent to his will, but as time passed, "there began to grow up a spirit of rebellion, on her part, a desire to judge for herself sometimes." Aylmer could not brook independence, and the couple became estranged. "Those pleasant little courtesies, which serve to keep love burning brightly on the domestic altar, were by degrees utterly neglected, and the lamp of love grew dim." The birth of a "beautiful babe" caused a reconciliation. "Husband and wife seem drawn together by this little golden link, and while the little angel gladdened their home, happiness remained."

Unfortunately the little angel flapped her wings prematurely. After the death of the child, contentiousness returned, and the couple lived "in almost constant enmity—each heart hardened and cold." One day when they were supposed to attend "an evening party," Aylmer was out of sorts. To irritate his wife he said that he was not going to the party. "Vexed," Mrs. Aylmer replied that she would go without him, whereupon he forbade her to go. Carrie refused to obey Aylmer's command. After reiterating that she intended to go to the party, she turned away from her husband "and began to fondle her lap-dog." Enraged, Aylmer "smothered an oath" and flinging himself from the house, "went off to his club." Although she was no longer eager to go to the party, Carrie felt she had to attend, if only to assert her independence.

Later that night both Aylmer and Carrie regretted their rash actions. On returning from the club, Aylmer thought about his marriage and "began to see, at last, how he had wronged and injured the wife he should have cherished." For her part Carrie blamed herself for not being more submissive and tender. "I will beg her forgiveness; I will win back my darling's love," Aylmer said as he waited for Carrie's return. "She shall lie on my heart, as in the olden time." Alas, she soon lay in a coffin. As Carrie returned home, "tender thoughts of the husband, once so dear, stealing into her heart," a fire engine crashed into her carriage. "She was thrown violently forward, and all was darkness." Aylmer rushed to her side, but she was dead by the time he reached her. "Carrie Aylmer," Winnie Woodbridge wrote with *Peterson's* fashion-conscious readers in mind, "had never looked lovelier than now, when she lay there in her gala robes. Her dress of pale-blue silk, with its frost-work of lace and pearls, only made more pallid the rounded form, lately so full of life and health." "Words," the authoress continued, "cannot picture that strong man's agony. He flung himself beside the body, and his voice grew hoarse with pleading for one more look, one single word of forgiveness. Alas, none came!" Guilt and grief turned Aylmer into a wanderer. "Years afterward, a grave was dug by strange hands, in a far distant land. None there knew that the lonely, broken-hearted man whose last resting-place it was, had when alive, borne the name of Harry Aylmer and had spent his days, ever since that terrible night in vain remorse for that FATAL QUARREL."

On the back of the magazine Charles Peterson urged women to "GET UP YOUR CLUBS." To subscribers who organized small reading groups, he promised "the premium engraving, 'Washington at the Battle of Trenton.'" *Peterson's* was not the only club whose membership came to my attention in Houston. Time has not only changed fashionable dress but also changed the doings of ladies, freeing society's Carries from the domination of husbands, making them more adventuresome and self-sufficient. At the back of Coleman's closet, Vicki found a paperback entitled *Six-Way Sex Club.* Written by Norma Griffet but not listing either date or place of publication, the book described doings at *Le Bastion,* "a health club." The novel detailed the antics of Patty, Olga, and Radley, this last the owner of the club. Forty-nine sketches appeared in the book. The dress of characters was skimpy. Crinoline and cashmere did not decorate the shoulders of Patty or Olga. No one wore dresses with basque waists or pagoda sleeves. Nothing was vandyked, and butterfly bows and flounces didn't appear, albeit some dramatic flouncing occurred in the novel itself. When Radley first met Olga, she was not fresh from boarding school. She was, however, well schooled in intimate matters, and as Radley stared at her, he thought how pleasant it would be to "give her a nice porking." *Six-Way Sex Club* would not appeal to vegetarians. The novel did not contain recipes for green corn soup or mock oyster fritters. Instead, the scenes served were meaty, on the raw side of uncooked, smacking of steak tartare. Still, Vicki and I read selections aloud. Cleaning house exhausted us, and the readings affected us much like a dose of Helmbold's Catawba Grape Pills. Indeed, the novel so perked up evenings that I almost wish I had a warren of aged uncles, all living in diverse cities and clamoring for help, their closets tenderloins of rare books.

What Vicki and I did in Houston was thankless. After I returned to Storrs, Amanda's nephew telephoned. He asked what happened to the antique furniture. An estate agent sold the furniture, making money enough both to repay the $9,317 I had already spent on Coleman and to cover nursing home expenses through November. Next, the man asked about Amanda's jewelry. In a plastic container I found four teeth containing gold fillings, Coleman's college fraternity pin, and three rings, from the settings of which jewels had been pried loose. At the bottom of a box of tie clasps was a Masonic medallion half an inch square. In the center of the medallion a gold crown circled a red cross. Attached to the top of the medallion was the head of a knight, a ruffle jutting from his neck and a visor pulled over his face. Engraved on the back of the medallion were "Sam Pickering" and "Carthage, Tenn." In the house I did not find silver or gold bracelets, pins, wedding rings, or strings of pearls. Neither did I discover certificates of deposit or keys to safety deposit boxes. After Mother died, Amanda came to Nashville and carted away two closets of dresses. None of the dresses were in the house in Houston. "What did you do with the bag of coins?" the man asked. "What coins?" I said. "The three or four hundred coins dating from the 1840s to the 1860s that Coleman kept in the chest in the living room," the man explained. "There was no bag of coins," I said. "Amanda's nephew must think," I said to Vicki after putting down the telephone, "that I have stolen everything." "No good deed ever goes unpunished," Vicki said, quoting the old platitude.

Prowling rooms at night and filling trash bags distracted me from concerns of the day. I spent much time in Houston on the telephone, one morning, for example, arranging to have the gas, electricity, water, and telephone cut off. At the Houston National Bank I set up an account entitled Samuel Francis Pickering Agent and Attorney in Fact for Coleman Enoch Pickering. Paying Coleman's bills from Storrs, then reimbursing myself, would produce a confusing paper trail, and I established the account so the banking record would read like a primer. From a checkbook I learned that Coleman received eleven hundred dollars a month from Social Security and his pension. The checks were mailed to the house and deposited by the yard man. I arranged to have the checks sent to the new account. The task was difficult. Government employees instructed me to bring Coleman to their offices to sign papers. Coleman could barely get out of bed, much less wander government buildings in downtown Houston. Snags were so many and so sharp that I considered abandoning the pension and Social Security. But then I talked to two compassionate government employees, both women. "Mr. Pickering," one said, "if you go by the rules, you will never be able to get your uncle's Social Security deposited in that account. The government doesn't exist to help people who are trying to be kind. Let me tell you what to do." The woman then suggested that I call the Social

Security Office in Washington and arrange for Coleman's check to be deposited directly into the account. "You will have to pretend that you are your uncle," she said. "The man there will ask you some personal questions," she continued, "but here is what they are." Another government employee told me how to arrange for the direct deposit of Coleman's pension. "Get form 1099A from the bank," she instructed, adding, "you will have to sign your uncle's name a couple of times. But you will just have to do that if you want to help him." "Jesus," Vicki said later, "you will go to jail because you helped a stranger. We would have been better off to have let Coleman die."

Longfellow was wrong when he wrote, "Lives of great men all remind us / We can make our lives sublime." It is not to those the world labels great to whom one should look for inspiration, but to the ordinary. At Sears Vicki and I had trouble finding trousers that would fit Coleman. On learning that we were buying clothes for an aged uncle, a sales girl was marvelously helpful. "Last week," she volunteered, "good trousers were on sale for two dollars and fifty cents. They are better than those that cost forty-five dollars." Not all the trousers sold, and the girl rummaged through the store room and found two pairs. An employee of GTE arranged for Coleman to have a telephone installed. The man and I chatted for a long time. I described the difficulties I encountered while trying to order Coleman's life, and he told me about his "baby sister" who suffered "bad with cirrhosis." The man tried to give Coleman a number I would remember. The last four digits were 2201, the twenty-two, he explained, being the number on the uniform of Emmitt Smith, a running back for the Dallas Cowboys football team, the zero followed by a one "standing for his being the best back in the National Football League." The man also advised me to block the line, so Coleman could not call eight or nine hundred numbers. The human buzzard is a lower animal than its ornithological cousin, and more often than not feeds upon the living rather than the dead. Thieves, the man said, contacted old people, even in nursing homes, and tried to steal money, often asking old people to call eight or nine hundred numbers.

After the trip in March, I considered bringing Coleman to Connecticut and placing him in a home in Storrs. The cost was seventy-two thousand dollars a year. A good nursing home in Houston was half the price. Until Coleman's house sold, I planned to pay his expenses. Consequently, instead of raiding my savings and perhaps having to borrow money, I did the easier and more convenient thing. I placed Coleman in a home in Houston. The simple sentences that fill lines and form a compact paragraph on a page distort life. Life sprawls through margins; thoughts dangle and blunder; the doings of one day erase the doings of another. Few of Vicki's and my conversations formed coherent wholes. One hour we pondered buying another house in Storrs, one large enough to contain both Coleman's and our lives. The next moment we thought about decamping, leaving Houston and letting heat and starvation end what they began.

Neighbors recommended several nursing homes, and after driving over Houston, I settled on a home in a residential area, seventeen and a half miles from Coleman's house. Prints of birds hung on walls. Carpets were thick and gold. Crepe myrtle bloomed in open courtyards, and in the dining hall yellow cloths lay atop tables. Several times Vicki and I explained the move to Coleman. He was too old to understand, and he accepted the move out of lethargy. After leaving him at the home the first day, we felt sorry for him, and both of us became teary. "You have done the best thing for him," Vicki said as I drove back to Coleman's house. Vicki was right. Air-conditioning and good meals changed Coleman.

Two days later when Vicki and I returned to the home, Coleman was talkative, and family stories spilled out of him like pages falling from a book so long shut the binding had rotted. Despite selling insurance Grandpa Pickering, I learned, never drove a car. The one time he tried to drive he crashed into the garage, shattering the door. Grandma, Coleman said, was a fine singer, a contralto who performed at funerals throughout Smith County. I learned that Coleman had been valedictorian of his high school class and that Father had played the piano, eventually stopping because he "didn't have any musical sense." Coleman said his parents spoiled him. He remembered gathering chestnuts at Chestnut Mound and almost stepping on a rattlesnake at Red Boiling Springs. When Vicki hung pictures on the wall, Coleman flirted with her. "If she were southern," he said, "she wouldn't work so hard. She'd just sit." Coleman told me he had been a good baseball player, a pitcher and a center fielder. Suddenly he reminded me of Edward, who pitched and played center field. Despite the rapid improvement, though, Coleman remained eighty-five years old, a recluse who had rarely left his house during the past four years. As a result many of the pages that tumbled into conversation were foxed. Coleman shared the room with another man. "That man," Coleman whispered, "is a tough one. He was a sheriff. He killed three men, so I am being careful." The man, I learned later, had been an accountant.

"What have we done?" Vicki said that afternoon. "Coleman is going to live forever. Suppose he outlives you. I don't know how to manage financial things." Since placing Coleman in the home, the sands of time occasionally resemble boulders. Not a day passes without my doing something for him. His life has become my life. Twice a week I write Coleman, not just resembling but becoming Grandmother. Last month I canceled two life insurance policies worth five thousand dollars apiece. I was the beneficiary of both policies. Coleman had neglected the policies. As a result interest on unpaid fees reduced their value. Canceling the policies took time and a file of letters. Ultimately, though, Coleman received $1,750.91, a goodly portion of a month's payment to the nursing home. Next Tuesday Coleman has an operation on his left eye. Without the operation, he will go blind. Monday I took out a year's subscription in the Houston newspaper for him. Tuesday I bought him a magnifying glass. After dinner I wrapped it in plastic bubbles. Wednesday I mailed it to Houston. Yesterday I learned that his property taxes were overdue.

Coleman did not like the sheriff and has moved to another room. "He gets along better with his new roommate," a nurse told me this afternoon, "although some days he threatens to kill him." Vacation is over. Last week I mailed the *Six-Way Sex Club* to an acquaintance. "I understand you are experiencing domestic chilblains," I wrote anonymously. "The enclosed is salubrious and inflaming. Two pages every night before bed will," I said, paraphrasing advertisements in *Peterson's,* "restore the fallen and invigorate the detumescent." "Summer may be over," Vicki said just now, walking into the room, "but Coleman's end lies beyond the horizon. You and he have a long way to go together before you glimpse the sunset." "Yes," I said, "that's the way it's going to be." "But," I continued, suddenly remembering the first lines of a poem in *Peterson's,* "Come, sing to me of sterling love, / A wild and gladsome strain; / To fall like sunshine from above, / That dances on the main."

SOMEBODY ELSE'S MAIL

"Well," I said to Vicki after I passed through Shepherd, north of Houston, and was finally able to relax behind the steering wheel, "my family now consists of one hamster, two dogs, three children, one wife, and one uncle." Vicki and I spent most of July in Texas ordering the affairs of Uncle Coleman. For months Coleman had been the subject of dinner table conversation and bedtime worry. Before leaving Houston, I settled him in a nursing home. "I have shaken loose," I said, sliding back in the seat, loosening my grip on the wheel and watching my knuckles turn pink again. "At least I have escaped Coleman for four days." "Yes," Vicki said, "but mail will be waiting for you in Connecticut, and you will pay for this break just as you must pay for boarding the animals." The trip was expensive. Eighteen days of room and board for Dusty the hamster cost fifty-four dollars while that for the dogs amounted to two hundred and forty-four dollars. Additionally, the children attended camp in Maine. They went to camp during previous summers, but this year they had to go so Vicki and I could travel to Houston. Room and board for the children made me howl, even scurry about like Dusty on his exercise wheel. A dozen speeches, a magazine rack of articles, and royalties for nine books only paid twenty-nine percent of camp fees.

Back in Storrs, however, I did not think about the children. A bundle of mail waited for me. Most of the mail referred to Coleman's affairs and required answers. Day after day notices from banks, a pension fund, the nursing home, pharmacies, doctors, and the federal government arrived, each, if not unexpected, at least forcing me to solve a jigsaw puzzle, the parts of which lay scattered amid a filing cabinet of papers. Occasionally parts were missing, and I fashioned solutions, hoping not only that the fabrications would fit but also that no bureaucrat would detect them. Instead of being peripheral to life, mail became central. Coleman's affairs so drained my energy that my own doings became incidentals: bulk mail, an assortment of catalogs and flyers, matter to occupy a glance but not thought.

I organized days around the mail. Not only did I anxiously await the delivery each day, but I also did chores in the mornings so I would have afternoons free for Coleman's affairs. Mail dominated the metaphors of everyday life as my mind seemed to resemble a mailbox, cluttered and overflowing. To accommodate Coleman's correspondence, I simplified days and found another home for Dusty. Dusty belonged to Eliza. Because he was nocturnal, usually waking up when Eliza was asleep, I cared for Dusty, taking him for scurries in the yard and cleaning the aquarium in which he lived. In June when I mentioned giving Dusty away, Eliza cried. On Eliza's return from camp, I packaged a proposal, wrapping it in seductive words, a technique I learned while writing letters on Coleman's behalf.

"Eliza," I said, strolling into her room, "how would you like a new porcelain doll? Look through *Dolls Magazine* and see if you can find a friend, a nicely dressed one costing around a hundred dollars." Before Eliza replied, I said, "One slight problem does exist. The dolls in the magazine are allergic to hamsters, and if you decide you want one, Dusty will have to move." The summer having taught me how to skin cats, even those with fur permanently stitched on by regulation, I knew discovering new digs for Dusty would be easy. In fact, that morning I talked to the mother of Megan, the little girl who cared for Dusty while we were in Texas. "Megan," she said, "would love Dusty." "Daddy," Eliza said, pulling the magazine from her bookshelf, "let me think about the doll." The next morning I ordered Mary Elizabeth, one of the Georgetown Collection. That afternoon Dusty went to live with Megan. "You spent one hundred and thirty dollars on a doll in order to get rid of a hamster that cost eight dollars?" Vicki asked, exasperation thick in her voice. "Damn straight," I said, "and I would have spent a hundred more if Eliza had balked." "What sort of lesson do you think you taught Eliza?" Vicki said. "No lesson," I said. "I acted expediently. Most actions don't mean. The right sort of people live simply. They pay little attention to instructions and don't beat through days flushing out lessons. Eliza has a doll. Dusty is gone, and that's that."

I ended the conversation like a man sealing a letter. Instead of pasting tape across an envelope, I slapped words firmly over the experience, then dropped it out of mind. Responsibility for Coleman filled days, reducing events, making them seem letters, experiences so self-contained that they appeared meaningless, the papery stuff of advertisement. One morning early my friend Josh appeared in the English department. "Read this," he said, handing me the woman's page from a newspaper. Josh had circled an article on "pregnancy envy." "Gas," Josh exclaimed. "Only men bloated by beans or a diet of the *au courant* suffer from pregnancy envy." Josh has little use for psychology. "The only envy that really exists," he continued, "is penis envy. Even then that fool Freud got things backward. Women don't turn green from penis envy. Men do. Many times in the shower in the gymnasium I've looked at the guy next to me and thought 'I wouldn't mind having that.'"

Josh's ideas are inflammatory. After he left the building, I decided to go home and see what Vicki thought about the matter. Vicki is not overly curious, or envious, and I suspected the topic would not intrigue her. Be that as it may, however, I did not subject her to an intellectual examination. The mail had arrived early. "Dear Mr. Pickering," Wayne Roxbury wrote Coleman from Hong Kong, "I was told that you can be trusted and that you are interested in legally making a great deal of money. While I was working with my company's super computer, I discovered a way of winning a lottery that regularly pays $6,000,000.00. Unfortunately, if the company finds out about it, they could use the system I developed to get the money for themselves.

"If you want some big money, here's what I propose," Roxbury continued. "I will send you the name of the lottery and the winning numbers generated by the computer. You play these numbers and we'll split the winnings 50/50 (up to $3,000,000.00 each, the first time alone). We don't have to stop there! We can do it many times—as long as we keep it secret. When you get the money, I will instruct you where to send my half. To show my confidence in the system that I developed, if you play the numbers that I give you in the lottery that I name and don't win, I'll give you $1,000.00 out of my own pocket. To show your sincerity, I ask you to mail me One Hundred U.S. Dollars ($100.00). Better yet, send the $100.00 cash, check, or money order, payable to Wayne Roxbury, by UPS or Federal Express. It will get here in a couple of days and can never get lost. If you are sending cash, be sure *not* to tell UPS or Federal Express that there is cash in the envelope, or they will refuse to take it. If you use ordinary air mail, you must put at least 60 cents postage on the envelope for it to reach me. To make sure you get my address right, I have enclosed a self-addressed envelope. Unless you use UPS or Federal Express, it takes about a week for mail to arrive in Hong Kong from the U.S. If I do not hear from you in ten days, I will find somebody else who wants to make a fortune."

If I could have thrust my hand into Mr. Roxbury's trousers, I would have grabbed jewels, not dollar bills. Every day people age into financial irresponsibility. The clasp of reason loosens, and savings spill out. Sharpers had long fed upon Coleman's assets. During the past two years, so far as I could make out, twenty thousand dollars had vanished from Coleman's savings, much disappearing down the maws of shady financial entrepreneurs. Coleman purchased tickets in European lotteries and bought stock in companies mining gold and titanium. His name must have appeared on a mailing list of aged suckers. Every day the mail brought him fabulous offers to enrich himself. "SILVER, SILVER, SILVER," one merchant wrote, offering to sell him coins. "I've found them," the man said, "but not enough for everyone."

When I first began teaching, a professor at Dartmouth said, "think the best about people, Sam, and they will give you their best." Often Coleman's mail gave the professor the lie. "Think the best of people," the mail taught, "and they will steal from you." "The man who pats the scorpion deserves punishment," Josh told me. To purge bile, I went for a walk after reading Roxbury's letter. Although summer had been dry, my spirit budded after only a few minutes outside. At the edge of a cornfield flower-of-an-hour bloomed, its deep purple eyes surrounded by petals so pale they seemed powdered. While I knelt looking at the pink stems of thorny pigweed, sixteen turkeys wandered out of a thicket. A tablecloth of Queen Anne's lace unrolled along a path. Earlier in the summer a raccoon dug turtle eggs out of a sandy hillside, scattering the eggshells. Dried, the shells resembled collapsed puffballs. The raccoon did not eat all the eggs. Under a layer of dirt at the bottom of the hole lay four small eggs. I opened one in hopes of finding a piece of turtle shell. The egg was a ball of maggots. I counted eleven before I stopped.

In the Ogushwitz meadow purple seeped out of joe-pye weed, and flowers turned brown. Instead of reaching to my chin goldenrod was waist-high. Except for thin puddles the beaver pond was dry, broad-leaf arrowhead blooming in the bed of the pond, drawing the eye and seeming to cinch banks above the pond together like buttons on a coat. Unnamed Pond still held water, and I sat under a willow and watched a pair of yellowlegs forage the shallows. When I walked around the pond, I stumbled upon a northern water snake clasping a green bullfrog in its mouth. I startled the snake, and it dropped the frog, wrinkled under the water, and vanished in a cloud. For a moment the frog hunched silent on the bank, then gathered itself and sprang into the mud. "The frog must have thought me a god," I told Vicki; "some day the good book *Rana* will describe how divine intervention saved Brother Catesbeiana from a serpent."

Religion was on my mind. Coleman probably dumped as much money into suspect collection plates as he shoveled into bottomless titanium mines. Christian bookies number the golden feathers on a fat goose, and before a single bird tumbles off the roost they try to pluck his bank account bare. Not satisfied with primary and secondary feathers, one charity pinched down, telephoning Coleman in the nursing home and asking for a donation. Coleman pledged money, and the charity billed me. My response was brusque, mentioning both money changers in the temple and the attorney general of Illinois. Every mail brought begging letters. "Lepers Reach Out with Special Needs," a flyer declared; "Time Is Short. We Must Have the Support of Concerned Christians Right Now!" "Mt. Pinatubo Erupts & Releases Huge Flow of Molten Lava," stated another flyer; "Philippine Countryside Left with Large Path of Utter Destruction! 300 Children Left Either Orphaned or Abandoned!" "Christian Booklets" cost "Only $12 a dozen—envelopes included," one organization advertised. Among the titles were *The Cross Is God's Christmas*

Tree, He Is Coming Again, and *The First Person to Doubt the Virgin Birth.* "Mary was the first person to question virgin birth," a note following this last title explained before adding, "How can this be?"

"Sowing and Reaping is still very much a part of God's Plan for Man," a preacher declared. "You are in the sowing business today, reaping time is part of your tomorrow. Make decisions in the light of this truth and this will be the best insurance policy you have ever taken out. Take fire into your bosom and YOU WILL BE BURNED. Open your heart to doing what is right, and Scriptural and spiritually correct and YOU WILL BE BLESSED!" "In the light of some of the contents of this letter," the man said at the conclusion of his sermon, "we have a special gift offer to make to you at this time. If you are one of our SPONSORS you may have our Cassette Tape Message on 'Divorce' upon your request. If you are not a SPONSOR (SPONSORS give at least $100 a year to our ministry) you may request this tape for a gift of $4.00." In Houston I found scores of tapes. None had been played. Coleman did not own a tape player. "On that tomorrow when stones swim and twigs sink," Josh advised me, "your suspicions about religious solicitations may be proved wrong and you will reap fire. Until then, however, distrust Christians bearing gifts and remain a rationalist of little faith." My essays describe more good religious goings-on than the *Pentateuch.* Nevertheless, if people from Carthage had not sent me postcards crammed with gossip about Old Testament doings, I might have booted faith out the back door. Proverbs Goforth told Slubey Garts that he reckoned the dove sent from the ark ought to have plucked a magnolia leaf. "Noah was one of the giants of the earth," Proverbs explained, "and no olive leaf, nor even a fig leaf, was big enough to cover his sweet vine."

Sickness, as the saying puts it, arrives on horseback and departs on foot. Daily I wrote doctors or telephoned the nursing home. Medicinal matters dismounted and made themselves so much a part of my hours that I could not escape the sickroom even when I visited characters inhabiting my essays. Googoo Hooberry had so serious a case of erysipelas that Doctor Sollows put him in the hospital. "This bacteria has laid me out," Googoo said when Hoben Donkin visited him. "Oh, there's nothing worse," Hoben responded, smoothing his hair down with his right hand; "I tore up my bacteria last fall lifting a damp bale of hay, and I had to lie flat for five days. Even now my rump tingles, almost as if I sat in something nasty and caught an infection." For the fourth straight year Lily June Humboldt had a child out of wedlock. Ray Cobb in Byrdstown fathered all the children. "Lily June," Doctor Sollows suggested after delivering the baby, "why don't you marry Ray? He's a good fellow." "He's solid, Doctor Sollows, and I've done thought about it," Lily June said, "but to tell the truth, he just don't appeal to me."

Apart from the hours I spent tending Coleman's correspondence, the doings of my life resembled postcards, flat impressions associated with one or two lines scribbled across memory. Vicki and the children and I attended the first football game at the university. Although I remember nothing about the game itself, I recall Eliza's carrying a book with her, "an Emergency Packet," Edward dubbed it. The book was *Eight Cousins, or The Aunt Hill* by Louisa May Alcott. Near the end of the third quarter Eliza finished the book. As we walked beside Hillside Road after the game, Vicki said, "life's football fever has begun again."

The next week I attended an open house at the middle school. I spent the afternoon and early evening working on Coleman's finances. My ledgers did not balance, so I decided to skip the formal program at the school. Unlike other parents who attended an assembly and followed a schedule, I darted through halls and in and out of rooms, breathlessly introducing myself to Eliza and Edward's teachers. Eliza accompanied me, "just to get in shape for soccer," she said later. Only once did I pause during the evening. On the linoleum floor outside Room 104, Eliza spotted "Albert the ant." "He's going to get squished, Daddy, if you don't take him outdoors," she said. As I had done for both Coleman and Dusty, I found Albert a new home, this one on the trunk of a shagbark hickory.

Education, conservative politics, and "biblical" Christianity were the subjects of much of Coleman's mail. The three coiled together, resembling a social ménage à trois. A broadside announced a "political rally" held at Liberty Revival Church outside Houston on State Highway 249. The guest speakers came to Texas, the flyer declared, "with an action-oriented agenda on how you can help restore American government to its Biblical premises and Constitutional boundaries." From Coleman's house in Houston I removed bales of political pamphlets, most sent from groups, which I regarded from my Connecticut point of view as, at best, on the social fringe. "Lie down with dogs, and you will get fleas," Mother often said. The matters to which Mother referred were fleshly not political. Nevertheless I indulge in safe politics and have never bedded down with, as Josh labels them, "the great unreasonable." Scrolled across the top of one pamphlet was "LESS GOVERNMENT, MORE RESPONSIBILITY, AND— WITH GOD'S HELP—A BETTER WORLD." Coleman subscribed to *The New American*, a magazine published by the John Birch Society. In August the post office stopped forwarding the magazine from Houston. Soon afterward the magazine was sent directly to my address. "You are on a little list," Vicki said, prancing into the study one night, paraphrasing Gilbert and Sullivan's *Mikado*.

In Coleman's mail education and Christianity scratched along comfortably together, rarely raising a hint of a constitutional blister. A "Christian School" advertised a book that revealed the socialist bias of American education. Education in the United States was, the advertisement stated, being restructured so that it would resemble "the *international / global* educational program of the *United Nations.*" "*Outcome / based learning,*" as proposed by the Department of Education, the advertisement warned, "*was implemented in Eastern Europe.*" Study of the proposed restructuring of American education revealed "an interlock with a small, but dedicated, body of people who have consistently worked to establish a single world government or a 'New World Order,'" one that would "ultimately result in the *compromise of national sovereignty.*"

That night I attended an open house at E. O. Smith High School. As Vicki and I visited Francis's classrooms, I looked for signs of educational restructuring. Pasted to a wall in the math room were several posters, all depicting Dalmatians, forty-six Dalmatians in fact. A region of Croatia, Dalmatia borders the eastern shore of the Adriatic Sea. Was this celebration of dogs, I wondered, an oblique indication of that learning which was first "implemented in Eastern Europe"? Also worrisome was the fact that the dogs, aside from collars and frilly ribbons, were naked. Moreover, many animals, primarily adolescents, curled fetchingly on, if not bear rugs, at least fluffy pillows, water bowls overflowing in front of them. Vicki is more robust than the educators nervous about national sovereignty. In Francis's English class we sat at student desks. "Look at this," Vicki said, pointing at the top of her desk. Someone had carved "Pussy" into the wood. "The New World Order is a long way off," Vicki said. "Unless the human male suddenly gets new ball bearings, life and education will splutter along as they have always done."

Vicki and I enjoyed the visit to the high school. We walked

home through the woods behind our house. Yellow stars nibbled at the blue night. The world seemed nice, and we laughed. The next day's mail, alas, turned the sky red, and made me long for a different order, anything but the vicious old, old order. Coleman received flyers from groups calling themselves the Sons of Liberty and the Christian Defense League. The Sons of Liberty sold books "TO PATRIOTS" wholesale. On their list were forty-three volumes, among others, *Construction of Secret Hiding Places, Roosevelt Warming the Serpent, Tracing Our White Ancestors (White Roots),* and then shelves of anti-Jewish tracts. *Octopus,* the advertisement explained, was "an exposé of the B'nai B'rith and the JDL as well as the Jew running America under Roosevelt." In *War, War, War,* Cincinnatus showed "how the Jews were behind almost every war in history." *World's Trouble Makers* proved that "the Jews have infiltrated and taken over major denominations of Christianity." For twenty dollars Coleman could buy a videocassette of *The Eternal Jew,* "the greatest movie ever produced exposing the *International Jewish* banking system and the real motives of the Jews toward the non-Jews of the world." "This film," the advertisement explained, "was mainly made in the Polish Warsaw Ghetto during the 1940s and it is not 'Jew Hollywood Quality' but the movie is clear and understandable. It was first produced in German and has English narration on it." After World War II, "the Jews had all known copies of this movie confiscated and destroyed." "Every patriot," the Sons of Liberty proclaimed, "should have a copy of this movie in his or her library," for it "completely tears away the veils on the Jewish quest for world conquest."

Never had soiling mail come to my house. Before I assumed responsibility for Coleman, the worst publication I received was the catalog for *Victoria's Secret.* After reading the flyers, I felt dirty. "Great-grandfather was wrong to fight for the Union," I told Vicki;

"the time has come for Connecticut to secede." The mail spoiled classes the next day. Instead of thinking the best of students, I suspected the worst. Brightness fell from the air, and I resented Coleman. I snapped at Vicki, and when Josh told me one of his silly puns, I didn't smile. "Why is hot bread like a caterpillar?" he asked. The answer was "because it's the grub that makes the butter fly."

Happily, responsibility did not allow me to luxuriate in anger. The next day's mail brought bills to pay for Coleman. Also in the mail was a letter from Miss Frances. Miss Frances lives in the Grand View Health Home in Danville, Pennsylvania. After reading an essay of mine describing turtles, she wrote me. I have never met Miss Frances, but we have corresponded for a decade and have become friends. "Daddy, why do you write someone who will never buy your books?" Edward once asked. "Are her letters interesting?" "Not especially," I said. "Well, then," Edward continued, "what do you get from the letters?" "Something, but I don't know exactly what it is," I said, ending the conversation. What I get, I now know, is goodness, the reassurance that if you think well of people, many will do their best for you. Miss Frances had not written me for some time because, as she put it, "poor health has rather taken over my living." Because her feet were "poor specimens these days," and she had "fallen a couple of times," she had learned to use a walker. Although writing was difficult, she wanted me to know that my friendship enriched her life. "I am so lucky," she wrote, "to have a friend such as you to be in touch with." After reading Miss Frances's letter, I went to Josh's office. "Josh," I said, "I really liked that pun yesterday. But did you read in the paper about the death of the man who led a rough life? He wanted to end things smoothly so he drank a quart of shellac."

For three days I stopped thinking about mail. Then one afternoon an advertisement from a funeral home arrived addressed to Coleman. Stamped in black type across the top of the advertisement were two questions. "If you died today, would your loved ones know your wishes?" "Would they even know what to do?" Listed in two columns beneath the questions were twenty-eight of "the 124 decisions," a Family Service Counselor said, "that must be made." Under the heading "Funeral Arrangements," survivors had, among other things, to select pallbearers, arrange embalming, choose a coffin, decide whether the coffin should be open during visitation hours, and in case it was open, pick out clothes for "the dearly beloved's wardrobe." "Wise people prepare for the future," the counselor advised, "and making final arrangements is part of that process!"

Being wise and responsible had tired me. Two days later I bolted the mailbox and, slipping the tether to Coleman, took Vicki and the children away from Storrs for four days. We spent two nights in both Salem and Rockport, Massachusetts. "Leaving the mail," Vicki said, "is like leaving Houston. I feel free." We roamed Salem, the names of streets, not that of my uncle, on our lips: Summer, Broad, Washington, Liberty, Hawthorne, Derby, and Orange. I walked out of worry into comfortable exhaustion. The children were endlessly energetic. "They wiggle like bugs in a crapper," Vicki said at the end of the first day. In Salem we stayed at the Salem Inn, a red-brick federal building built in 1834. Our room was the garret on the fourth floor, forty-three steps up, Eliza told me. We spent days visiting tourist sites: the Witch Museum, the House of Seven Gables, and the Peabody Essex Museum. While Vicki and the children toured the Wax Museum, I bought "hot" candy from a Fun Shop on the Essex Street Mall. In the middle of each piece of candy lay a nugget of mustard. "Here's a treat for you," I said, presenting a hunk of candy to each member of the family. Life in my family has more bite than any bon-

bon. Not once did Vicki or the children make a face. "The candy tasted peppery," Eliza said later, "but it was nothing like a fireball, and I like hot things."

We walked the length of Chestnut Street and amid the Federal mansions suffered private home envy. While tiffs about constitutional boundaries and outcome-based learning rarely provoke anything other than blather, private home envy influences thought, almost making me a sucker for a proposal from Wayne Roxbury. We visited the Pickering House on Broad Street, built in 1651 by John Pickering and bequeathed to his older son. Pickering's second son, my ancestor, lived elsewhere. Ten generations of Pickerings had inhabited the house. "Would you like to live here in the shadow of your forefathers?" Francis asked me. Googoo Hooberry suddenly came to mind. The Hooberrys had long thrived on the hills around Carthage, and when Googoo was in the hospital, Doctor Sollows asked him, "which of the Hooberrys were your forefathers?" "I don't know nothing about any four fathers," Googoo responded; "old man Titus Hooberry was my one father."

In Rockport I explored art galleries along South Road and Main Street. I chatted with painters in the Rocky Neck Art Colony in East Gloucester and dreamed of owning a painting by Fitz Hugh Lane, light shaking across Gloucester Harbor in luminous slats of yellow and silver. After leaving Rocky Neck, we went to the lighthouse at Eastern Point. Vicki drove so I could study mansions along the road. We almost missed the lighthouse. Near the point stone pillars stood on each side of the road. Stenciled in white on one pillar were the words "Private Property"; on the other appeared "No Trespassing." Instead of driving between the pillars, Vicki circled and started back to Gloucester. After Vicki drove a quarter of a mile, a red Plymouth hurried up behind us and started honking. Vicki pulled onto the shoulder of the road, and a woman jumped out of the car. "I saw you stop at the pillars," she explained, "and noticed that you were from out of state. You turn right around and go to the lighthouse. This is a public road. Don't pay any attention to the writing on the pillars. Some stinky rich people painted the signs on two weeks ago. They think they own this place, but they don't."

In describing dawn, Googoo said, "the sun rose all over the place." The trip to Massachusetts lifted my spirits. I knew Coleman would be my responsibility for a long time. Managing his affairs would be difficult, but so far I had handled things adequately and progressed beyond a learner's permit. As I drove back to Connecticut, the sun shone everywhere. Not much mail awaited me in Storrs, and life slipped into a familiar pattern. One morning Vicki and I and Mary, Roger, Ellen, and George, these last four friends from the Cup of Sun café, went to Caprilands, an herb farm in Coventry. Because lunch cost eighteen dollars a person, we did not eat. Instead, Ellen handed out oatmeal cookies, and we roamed the gardens nibbling herbs, my favorite being Sweet Annie.

In a greenhouse a woman told me that pennyroyal kept fleas away. In the fall at home children, not fleas, raise bumps of wordy irritation. Each morning while Edward and Eliza wait at the end of the driveway for the schoolbus, Vicki stands by the kitchen door. One morning not long after we returned from Massachusetts Eliza yelled at Edward and swung her backpack at him like a scythe. She missed, but Edward threw his pack at her, hitting her on the bottom and scattering his lunch under the peonies. Vicki had gotten up at six o'clock to prepare the lunches. For a moment Vicki stared at the children. Then she spoke to herself. "You want to fuck, and you do it, and then you have all these years of turmoil." "Well," I said, changing my plans for the morning, "I think I'll go swimming."

That afternoon I picked Edward up at the middle school when he finished soccer practice. Edward practiced soccer on Monday, Tuesday, Wednesday, and Thursday afternoons. On weekends he played two games, one always on Saturday, the other always on Sunday. Eliza's schedule was not so rigorous. She only practiced twice a week, not at school, however, but at Lions Field on the other side of town on Wednesday and Friday evenings at six o'clock. Like Edward she played two games on the weekend, one on Saturday, the other on Sunday. Not only did Vicki and I spend weeks driving, but since games were often played in distant towns, we had to stay and watch. Soccer bound other families in Mansfield to the same schedule. On sidelines families mulled the effects of soccer, not complaining but pondering the influence of sport upon children. When two mothers at the middle school began to discuss how soccer affected their boys, I interrupted. "Soccer," I said, "has little effect upon children. They are too young to be influenced by anything. Soccer has changed the lives of parents, not progeny." Soccer had stepped up, I explained, using language appropriate to athletic endeavors, to fill the moral gap created by religious decline. Not belief but soccer imposed order on the lives of breeding adults. Driving children so filled parents' days that they had no time to sport about themselves. "An absolutely charming lady scholar in the sociology department at the university had," I continued, "recently completed a study of the effects of soccer upon adults in Mansfield. During the last five years among parents of soccer-playing children, adultery has declined 76.81%." When one mother stepped backward, I trapped the topic and took off on a breakaway. "Not only that," I said, "the divorce rate among parents capable of indiscriminate mating has plummeted. Of course the effects of creating separate teams for girls and for boys have not been calculated. I, for example, have been privy to liaisons of men with men, relationships that would never have been formed in the old days when religion and adultery flourished."

"How was practice?" I asked Edward when he got into the car. He was glum and muttered "all right." Edward's moodiness did not bother me. The anxiety blown over my life by Coleman's mail had lifted. When we got home, Vicki was waiting by the kitchen door. "Your flowers arrived," she said, pointing to two cardboard boxes. The boxes contained four hundred daffodil bulbs: Redhill, Las Vegas, Hillstar, Daydream, Jetfire, and Winston Churchill. Each fall I plant bulbs in the dell next to the house. Planting is difficult. Stones roll through the dirt in great wheels. Before placing the bulbs in the ground, I pry stones loose and cart them to a rock pile after which I fill the holes with compost dug from the woods. "They will be lovely in spring," Vicki said, sitting on a stump while I smoothed dirt atop the last bulbs; "we will have to take pictures and send them to Coleman. That way he will have some nice mail." "Yes," I said, rubbing my hands down the front of my trousers.

BOOK TOUR

Reading occasionally influences life. In the *Hartford Courant* I read an article describing a book tour made by Kaye Gibbons. To publicize her novel *Sights Unseen,* Gibbons visited thirty cities. *Walkabout Year,* my latest collection of essays, appeared in early October. "Damn," I said to Vicki, putting the paper down on the kitchen table, "I bet my Australia book would sell better if I went on a tour." "Then go on one," Vicki said, bending over and slipping a tray of cinnamon buns into the oven. I followed Vicki's advice. I walked out of the kitchen into the hall. From a hook in the closet, I removed the Akubra hat that I bought in Cairns three years ago. Then I strolled through the woods to the Cup of Sun, the first stop on my tour. I drank two cups of coffee, ate a bran muffin, and talked to Mary, Ellen, George, and Roger. Later that morning Eliza played soccer at Spring Hill. I wore the hat to the game. "Just in from the outback?" Chuck said when he saw me. "No," I said, "I'm on a book tour, and this is my second appearance." "Oh," Chuck said, pausing before asking, "do you think the girls will win today?" "Yes," I said. I watched the game. The girls won 4-0. When I returned home, I hung the Akubra back on the hook in the closet. The tour was over, or at least the actual tour ended. My imaginary tour, however, was in full swing, stretching not just through thirty cities but through all my days, not only shaping sights unseen but so quickening them that they cast bright shadows across the hours.

Children force parents to see clearly. In a family the sun often rises and sets at high noon, preventing parents from dreaming and transforming shadows into the stuff of life. Recently the president of the United States spoke at the University of Connecticut. "Daddy," Eliza said at dinner one night, "the parents of lots of my friends received invitations to meet the president. You write books. Why weren't you invited?" Before I answered, Edward spoke. "Many people write books," he said; "Dad's not important." Edward told the truth, something that brings book tours to abrupt ends. Because my applications are always rejected, I no longer apply for literary fellowships. Now, instead of becoming gloomy as I fill out forms and realize that no matter my words the applications will fail, I only dream of success. I imagine the pages fellowships will enable me to write. When I get up from my desk after not completing an application, I feel invigorated. I am ready to wander hill and field and spinning loops through the air turn falling leaves into necklaces, strings of jewels: yellow sugar maple and black locust, crimson red maple, orange hickory, and bronze beech. Keeping imagination vital is not easy. This fall I turned down two speaking engagements because the fees offered were modest. In contrast I agreed to speak on four occasions for free. "The honorariums were so low they made me feel ordinary," I explained to Vicki. "When a person doesn't receive a fee, he is free to create an imaginary self. Money does not define him and reduce him to the everyday." "But," Edward said when I finished the explanation, "if you made the speeches, you would earn enough to buy Mommy the new refrigerator she wants."

Writers whose tours take them to faraway places meet lots of literary folk. On my tour I met only one other writer, and that was Eliza. On Eliza's desk I found an account of Hungry Bert, a young vole who spent his summer playing games instead of stocking a larder for the winter. During the first week of winter Bert stripped the shelves of his storeroom. Forced to leave his burrow to search for food, Bert suffered from the cold. "'Just look at my hands; they are frozen,' Bert exclaimed; 'even the marrow of my bones is blue from cold!' 'That's what you get from playing kick-the-acorn instead of collecting insects for the winter!' cried a goose, flying south." Luck enabled Bert to survive "the winter of '93," as Eliza phrased it. Early in the fall a squirrel abandoned a flea-infested nest. In a corner of the nest Bert discovered a cache of acorns.

In late September fleas infested our yard. In jumping from the grass to George and Penny, they hopped into dinner table conversation. From there they bounced into Eliza's writings. While cleaning Eliza's room, I found a poem under the bed. The poem was entitled "Poppies." "The poppies grow gaily out upon the green, / Their colors are sapphires and a rosy sheen. / They bob and dance so gracefully in the blowing breeze, / While listening to the music and singing with the fleas. / If I were but a poppy in a field of grass, / I know a flute I'd play, not a horn of brass."

After book tours writers often get mail. Despite the appearance of *Walkabout Year,* I received few letters this fall. Only after my tour ended did the mail bring letters that touched on writing matters. One day I received two letters. Announcing the publication of a magazine devoted to elementary school matters, the first letter began, "Dear Literature Professional." An old friend and a literary amateur who had written a box of books wrote the second letter. Some time ago he suffered a stroke, and I wrote him, wishing him good health and describing the happy hours I spent watching the children play soccer. "Your soccer-parent days remind me of my son and me years ago," my friend said. "Now all my grandchildren are college graduates and ready to improve an imperfect world. Alas."

Unlike most writers on tour, schedule did not buckle me tightly to place and time. "Your tour," Vicki said, "sounds more like a detour." "Yes," I said, "that's the best kind of tour." One morning I drifted through Carthage, Tennessee. I didn't sign copies of my book, but I learned that Alice Blair, the fairest bud ever to bloom in the gritty soil around Mayflower, had married William Whicker from Nashville. Whicker was from a wealthy family. He grew up in a big house on Craighead and graduated from Wallace School after which he spent two lean years at Vanderbilt. Rich men often make poor husbands, and Whicker did not appreciate Alice, thinking her roots ran shallower than those of people blossoming in West Nashville. One night after she labored over dinner, Alice asked, "Darling, do I cook as well as your mother?" "My dear girl," Whicker responded, turning his fork sideways and digging at a kernel of corn lodged next to the first premolar on the left side of his face, "I come from an old and distinguished family. My mother was not a cook." Old and distinguished the Whickers may have been; brainy they were not. Before the wedding Whicker's brother Baxley visited the Blairs in Mayflower. Alice's father Nunnley was a deacon in the local church. On Sunday night Baxley accompanied Nunnley to a meeting of the church vestry. A parishioner had left the church a substantial bequest, and the vestry debated whether to spend the money on a chandelier or on a piano. Out of courtesy the vestry solicited Baxley's opinion. "If I was you," Baxley said, excavating a seam of golden wax running through his inner ear, "I'd buy a piano. You are mighty deep in the country, and you aren't going to find anybody out here who can play a chandelier."

Carthage itself enjoyed Indian summer, that quiet time between the last of the summer camp meetings and the first of the winter revivals. Taking advantage of the theological calm, Slubey Garts started a collection of sermons. "Folks tell that you are writing a book," Googoo Hooberry said to Slubey one afternoon. "Yes," Slubey answered, "although I'm just a poor weak worm creeping after Christ, I'm trying to do a little something at it." "Well," Googoo said, "keep going. You have just as much right to make a book as them that knows how." Slubey had not progressed far when I visited Carthage. He had decided on a title, written part of an invocation, and filled a spiral notebook with jottings. The title was *Like to a Saltlick,* the phrase being taken from "Come back to Christ like to a saltlick," an invitation Slubey often issued during services at the Tabernacle of Love, spreading his arms wide, gazing upward, and staggering slightly, looking like, Turlow Gutheridge said, "he was carrying a giant turnip to the Smith County Fair."

Slubey liked music. He often said, "you can lead a congregation to the collection plate but without some whooping and hollering they'll just stand there." In the invocation Slubey combined his affection for music with what he thought was the dangerous spread of Catholicism in Tennessee, particularly in Nashville. "After Nashville, Carthage; after Carthage, the world," Proverbs Goforth declared one Sunday. In the invocation Slubey stated that *papist* and *Romanist* disagreed not only with his soul but also with his ear. In order to make his prose more euphonic and more pleasing to God and man, he was changing, he wrote, the *-ist* ending of *papist* and *Romanist* to *-ite,* thus producing *papite* and *Romanite.* "Christ did not build his cathedral on a cabbage stump, but on words," Slubey said, explaining that in changing *-ist* to *-ite* he was following "the divine pencil." "Edomites, Moabites, and Ammonites," he said, wandered the Holy Land, "not Edomists, Moabists, and Ammonists." "Elijah was a Tishbite, not a Tishbist; Ephron was a Hittite, not a Hittist, and Bildad was a Shuite, not a Shuist." I told Slubey that I didn't think linguists would adopt his changes. But I could be wrong. After I told Josh about Slubey's proposal, he embraced the notion wholeheartedly and immediately began calling Communists, Communites, and feminists, feminites.

Despite the invocation Slubey's notes implied that the book would contain only one critique of papite practices. Under the heading "Relics and Bamboozle" appeared a list, "pickled tongues, candied noses, and ears in aspic" followed by "the hook that caught the great fish which swallowed Jonah, the bag from one of Pharaoh's lean kine, and three hairs from the tail of the ass that Jesus rode into Jerusalem." The rest of the sermons appeared to be standard moral fare. Under "Anger," Slubey wrote, "Describe the red-mouthed man." Beneath "Spewing Hate" *Humility* appeared, followed by "bowing to a dwarf will not prevent a man from standing up again." On another page, one that I assumed referred to Gluttony, he wrote, "John the Baptist fed on locusts, but today people are not satisfied with chocolate-covered raspberries or strawberries; they want chocolate-covered watermelons." "Lazy folks," he wrote on the next page, "water the horse with the milk bucket. In spring they don't drain fields, and instead of corn they raise frogs." Under "Ravages of Cupid," he warned, "bedroom slippers are made out of banana skins. Only wingtips can ferry the soul over the bottomless ocean of corruption." Watery metaphors lay beached throughout Slubey's notes. "Many lewdsters," he wrote, "awash on the flood of sin consider sending a note to God in a bottle, begging for help and forgiveness. Alas, wine fills all the bottles in their basements, and instead of praying to God they worship drink and sink under the waves." On the same page appeared an anecdote. Although Slubey ran a pencil through the names, I was able to decipher "Horace

Armitage" and "Enos Mayfield's Inn." Horace, it seems, appeared at the inn late one Saturday night. Drunk and short of money, he slapped a Gideon Bible on the bar "as security for drink." When Enos refused to accept the bible, Horace was incensed. "Why you refuse God's own word!" he shouted, staggering toward the door. "You must be an infidel."

My tour did not flow smoothly. Fatherhood forced me to return to Storrs for soccer games. On the Sunday of Columbus Day weekend, I got up at six o'clock in order to drive Edward to Lebanon for a tournament that began at eight. I returned home at 6:45 that evening, Eliza's last game having started in Willimantic at 5:10 in the afternoon. Sarah Dorr was Eliza's best friend. Sarah played on the same team as Eliza, and often I drove the girls to games. Afterward they enjoyed insulting each other, Eliza calling Sarah "doorknob" and Sarah responding with "nosepicker." When soccer did not kick books out of mind, Josh burst into my office. "Great god!" he exclaimed last Tuesday. "The woods are full of men in drag and carrying guns. Don't think about going on one of your inspirational little rambles now." "In drag?" I asked. "Yes," he said, "flaming queens in gray and green outfits." "Camouflage," I said; "the men are hunters dressed in camouflage." "No!" Josh shouted. "Soldiers wear camouflage, and no war is being fought in Mansfield. The men are queens." Early in October myth was on Josh's mind. "Remember Pygmalion," he said, "the sculptor who carved a statue of a beautiful woman and then fell so in love with his creation that he kissed it, whereupon the gods blessed him and turned her into flesh and blood?" "Sure," I said. "Supposedly, Pygmalion and his bride lived happily ever after." "Well," Josh continued, "that wouldn't happen in today's feminite environment. Now the statue would accuse Pygmalion of sexual harassment and sue him for kissing without permission."

Josh is fond of silly stories, and yesterday he insisted upon my listening to an account of a mother snake and her nineteen snakelings. The snakelings spent days practicing hissing, perfecting their technique in a pit dug for them by their mother. One day when the mother had to slither out to crawl a couple of errands, she sent her children to the den of Mrs. Pot, a neighbor. Mrs. Pot was out of her den, but when she returned and found the snakelings hissing in her pit, she sent them home. When they crawled through the front hole, the babies' mother asked why they came home so soon. "Mrs. Pot sent us," the snakelings cried. "Why that ungrateful coluber," the mother exclaimed. "Who assisted her the last time she suffered from ecdysis and couldn't see? Who nursed her when she bruised her fangs against the heel of man? Who does Mrs. Pot think she is? Her family is new to this range. Who showed her all the vole runs? Why I remember when the Pots didn't have a pit to hiss in."

I had heard Josh's story before. Instead of boring, however, repetition reassures, implying that life is comfortably circular, not linear. Yesterday's event will be tomorrow's happening, and no regimen of zeal or moral earnestness can alter the cycle. Rather than thrusting forward into the unknown, carrying banners proclaiming "progress" and "development," the person who believes life circular can relax, and riding the wheel of days, marvel at the dust pitched up by spinning time. On my tour I traveled a familiar October landscape. Fields appeared shaved, the corn stalks chopped into silage. From Horsebarn Hill the land rumpled outward in embers, trees flaming red and orange through ashy mists. In depressions between rows of stalks, lamb's quarters glowed, the stems claret and the flowers purple. Low bush huckleberry spilled down a slope in a red haze. Beneath leaves yellow crystals glittered like small sparks. In woods hayscented and New York ferns crumpled. Color leached out of fronds, transforming them into ghostly remnants of the green that rolled like water through spring. Down the hill behind the sheep barn cinnamon ferns turned ochre, looking as if they had been burned by a damp fire, cindered and rusted at the same time. Bundles of satiny sweet everlasting glowed in the dull light. Bushy and purple-stemmed asters drifted across vision looking as fragile as cirrus clouds. Canada geese honked overhead, the sound almost too familiar to hear. In contrast calls of crows jerked into awareness like wrenches tugging frozen bolts. A collar of alders pressed against the woods. Resembling gauze bandages, woolly aphids wrapped around twigs. The larvae of striped alder sawfly clung in circles to the margins of leaves and on cold mornings glistened like glazed doughnuts.

Leaves bunched across the forest floor in shag rugs. The foliage thinned. The woods turned yellow, and shadows became wispy. As sunlight sifted through black birch and sugar maple, it lost body and absorbing color floated lightly over the understory like a throw of weary lace. Thickets of spicebush turned hollows yellow. Along the border of the woods, green dried out of beaked hazelnut. For a moment the leaves turned yellow. Then splotches spread across them like measles, at first appearing red and proud but then shrinking into brown crust.

Because I had no appointments, I drifted across days. Instead of signing books, I looked for, if not the signatures, at least traces of others. On a dead star-nosed mole flies laid eggs in clutches, resembling bundles of shiny white spindles. Sagging on a spicebush were three heart-shaped balloons, all with "Happy Anniversary" printed on them. A hedge of pink hibiscus blossomed across the front of one balloon. On the second balloon horticultural artists forced peonies out of season and into the company of chicory and goldenrod. A wicker basket opened like a ventricle on the last balloon. Roses burst over the rim of the basket in scarlet spurts while in the middle of the basket a dove huddled on a nest, an anniversary being a time when home is where the heart is and when feeling pulses stronger than thought.

I followed whim through days. One damp morning I watched leaves drizzle into the Fenton River. Some surfed the air, riding up over a finger of breeze then quickly dipping and coasting into the water. Others swung through circles resembling drops tossed out by a sprinkler. Some leaves from red maples turned like corkscrews. Others with long stems fell like arrows. The river was low, and leaves drifted slowly downstream, bunching against rocks and ledges, and in worn bends rumpling together, resembling quilts pushed against headboards. Hemlocks grew along the river bank, and needles hooked leaves, seeming to reel them in and wear them as ornaments. I walked up from the river to the raspberry field. A woodcock broke cover and flying low circled behind me. A flock of yellow-rumped warblers hurried through the scrub. Sulfur shelf fungus bloomed on a log. The leaves of staghorn sumac resembled artists' palettes running with color, green near the stems, deep orange in the middle, and red at the tips. Northern red oak grew at the edge of the field. Color swept out from then drew back into the big leaves, shimmering, making me think Neats Foot oil had been rubbed into them. White pines towered behind the oaks. Tops of the trees were green, but nearer the ground branches had broken off, and the trunks resembled heavy culverts, at their bases needles oozing out in an overflow of orange.

To see how season signed October I toured at different times. Early in the morning fibrous mists floated over lowlands. A tuft of reed canary grass resembled a scythe, the panicle bending the stem into a blade. Inside the curve hung a spider web, droplets of water silver on the silk, creating the illusion of motion, making the grass swish through the air. A bumblebee quivered chilled and dying on top of a field thistle. Seeds spilled out of milkweed in damp mats, resembling sheets of water that had frozen, melted, and frozen again, this last time into cloudy sheaves. At midday I forced my hands into open milkweed pods. The pods felt warm and oily. Sometimes I shook stalks, and a frolic of clouds blew out of the pods. Below the white hairs seeds hung swollen, arches of yellow at the bases of the hairs curving over them like minute rainbows. On Queen Anne's lace umbrels folded inward so seeds could dry. Lady bugs nested in the umbrels, the prickly seeds blankets around them. I did not tell Josh or Slubey about touring early October. Queen Anne's lace, Josh would have warned, was just the bit of nifty to spice up the gowns of men trolling the woods with guns and dressed fit to kill, hoping for a slice of the old venison. Slubey would have preached to me, accusing me of turning nature into god. I can hear Slubey now. "Instead of listening to the rustle of leaves, harken to the rustle of angels' wings."

Book tours, as Slubey might have put it, "pry open the portals of the head." At the end of a tour writers return home, having seen and heard the stuff of new stories. One evening during the middle of my tour, I drove Eliza to soccer practice. As I drove along the dirt road past the town dump, Eliza asked a question. "Daddy," she said, "what is Communism?" "Communism was," I said, "a theory of government. Like all theories it promised people better lives." I explained that the gap between theory and practice was vast, primarily, I said, because humans were flawed creatures. Self always got in the way when people tried to implement theory. "Instead of being our brothers' keepers," I said, "we have become our brothers' exploiters." "Communism," I continued, promised "a fairer distribution of income. If the United States were a Communist country," I said, "I would not have the money to send you to Camp Wohelo in Maine each summer. But then

some of the poor children in Hartford might have better lives."
"That doesn't sound bad to me, Daddy," Eliza said. "I don't know why Americans hate Communism so much."

The practice field was four miles from our house, so I stayed at the field and talked to parents. Most parents were threads from the same financial and social fabric: doctors, teachers, lawyers, and artists. A few parents did not have means, however. On the weekend Eliza's team was scheduled to play in a tournament. The entrance fee for the tournament was fifteen dollars a child. "Is Sally looking forward to the tournament?" I said to a mother. "She'd like to play," the mother answered slowly, "but we can't come up with the fifteen dollars. Bill broke his arm six weeks ago. He hasn't worked since, and we don't have insurance." Sally played in the tournament. Afterward she baked me an apple pie. The pie was sweet. Still, as I ate it, my mind scrolled back to the conversation with Eliza. "Fifteen dollars," I thought, "from each according to his abilities. To each according to his need. Communites could teach us a lesson."

The narrative weather changed rapidly during my tour. While some stories were cloudy, others were sunny. The morning after the tournament I went to the Cup of Sun, and Ellen told me a story about Robbie, the five-year-old son of a friend. This fall Robbie started kindergarten. When he got on the bus the first day, he asked the bus driver his name. "Just call me Mr. Bus Driver," the man said. "Isn't it wonderful, Daddy," Robbie said to his father later, "that Mr. and Mrs. Driver named their little boy Bus, and when he grew up, he became a bus driver?" "Yes, son," the father said, "that's wonderful." As children age, stories told about them remain wondrous, albeit the tone changes. Edward's soccer team played most games on a field below the middle school. Parents parked cars at the school. We sat on a railing at the edge of the parking lot, watched the games, and talked about our children, then life itself. Twelve and thirteen, the boys on the team had grown prickly. "Ryan," a mother recounted, "never wears shoes out of the locker room. Last Wednesday when the temperature was below freezing, he walked barefoot across the parking lot. When he got to the car, he said, 'boy, I'm cold.' 'Maybe, if you wore your shoes, you would be warmer,' I suggested. 'Why are you always trying to ruin my life!' he shouted, getting into the back seat and slamming the door."

Halloween is a week away, and at the Cup of Sun this morning, friends and I dallied through muffins and coffee, talking about costumes. One year when I was a graduate student, I bought several pairs of inflatable buttocks. I strapped them to my chest and backside and went to a party as an ass. Another time I purchased a plague of rubber flies. I glued a swarm to my face. Afterward I attached threads to the wings of another swarm and hung them from the brim of a battered Cavanaugh hat. Then I went to a party as Fly Face, a character from the Dick Tracy comic strip. "Costumes are fun," Mary said; "years ago a friend convinced his sweetheart to dress like a girl scout for a Halloween party. She put the outfit on in my friend's apartment, and they never got to the party." "Sort of like your book tour," George said; "you never got out of Mansfield." "Still, I bet you had almost as much fun as that scout master," Ellen said. "More," I said. "I had much more fun."

INDOLENCE

"We do not know today whether we are busy or idle," Ralph Waldo Emerson wrote in *Experience.* "In times when we thought ourselves indolent, we have afterwards discovered, that much was accomplished." Idle hands write essays. For the essayist, meandering is work. Instead of rolling through days like a steam engine, the essayist shunts onto a siding. Far from timetable and straight and narrow rails, the essayist uncouples purpose. When a conductor shouts "all aboard," the essayist climbs on an imaginary train, one that clatters not over ties that bind but along sleepers. Guinea, Woodford, Penola, Rutherglen, Doswell, and Ashland are not stops in northern Virginia but imaginary places, towns where one drops a verb or preposition and takes on a paragraph.

The industrious man thinks the statement "curiosity killed the cat" cautionary, warning people to weld flanges on their thoughts so imagination does not pull them off the right of way, jerking them from the high trestle of conventional success into low unknowns. In contrast the idler wonders what the cat was curious about. For his part the essayist ponders cats themselves. Cats are not mentioned in the Bible. According to Macedonian tale, cats were banned from the Bible because a cat, not a snake, seduced Eve. The cat rubbed against Eve's legs, all the while mewing soft, flattering words that made Eve's flesh purr.

Biblical writers didn't celebrate idleness. Instead they urged people to copy the busy ant. While the soul of the diligent, Solomon declared, "shall be made fat," that of the sluggard would have "nothing." The idler was cousin to beggar and glutton. "Drowsiness," Solomon warned, "shall clothe a man with rags." Along with cats, divines banished tales that distracted from doctrine. According to another Macedonian story, Simeon gave the baby Jesus a chicken for a pet. The chicken stayed with Jesus until the Last Supper. When Jesus rode into Jerusalem on a donkey, the chicken perched on the animal's haunches and crowed. The chicken laid magical eggs. Biblical scenes decorated the shells: the water of Meribah flowing from the rock struck by Moses, Gideon threshing wheat by the winepress, and Elijah riding the whirlwind to heaven. So long as the eggs depicted ancient history, the chicken roosted well. Near the end of Christ's life, however, illustrations on the shells began to predict the future. After Judas discovered an egg showing him betraying Christ, the chicken's days were numbered. According to the story, Judas betrayed Christ not because of greed, jealousy, or the unbearable burden of associating with absolute goodness, but because one of his duties was cleaning after the chicken. Judas thought it ignominious that a grown man care for a bird. The night before the Last Supper Judas chopped the chicken's head off. The next morning Judas cooked the chicken and served it to the servants who waited on the disciples. After the servants picked the chicken clean, Judas buried the bones. Overnight the Judas tree sprang from the bones. When Judas committed suicide, he hanged himself from the tree. At Judas's death purple flowers blossomed like feathers on the tree, and Peter said that a perfumed wind blew through the tree, rattling leaves against branches, making a cackling sound.

Not in a hurry to accomplish, the idler has time for story. In October I spent several drowsy days in Carthage. A storm washed away a section of fence surrounding the Pillow of Heaven Cemetery. Repairs were expensive, so instead of replacing the broken section, Slubey Garts had the entire fence removed. "With so many people dying to get into the graveyard," Proverbs Goforth explained, "Slubey didn't think it right to keep the fence." Much as story wheezed through my prose, so railroads ran through Slubey's ruminations in October. One night Horace Armitage drank too much at Enos Mayfield's Inn. On the way home Horace fell into the Cumberland River and drowned. "When Horace boarded the gospel train, he headed straight for the club car," Slubey said on hearing about the accident. Slubey's sermons were sometimes too intellectual for the congregation at the Tabernacle of Love. One Sunday he mentioned "the voice of the turtle." "Slubey," Googoo Hooberry asked after the sermon, "what does a turtle sound like? Around my pond frogs talk something fierce, but I've never heard a turtle even whisper."

Googoo enjoyed a social October. His cousin Cerumen Hooberry visited him for two weeks. Cerumen lived in Castalian Springs and rode the bus to Carthage. "Did you meet Cerumen at the bus station?" Loppie Groat asked Googoo. "Meet him? Goodness me, no," Googoo said. "I've known him for years. He's been my cousin ever since I was born." Cerumen's ears were so plugged when he arrived in Carthage that Googoo took him to Doctor Sollows. The doctor prescribed drops containing sheep's gall. Ten days after Cerumen returned to Castalian Springs, Doctor Sollows met Googoo on Main Street. "Did that medicine cure your cousin's deafness?" Doctor Sollows asked. "Yes, indeed," Googoo said beaming. "I got a letter from Cerumen yesterday, and he told me that when he got home, he heard from a friend in Alabama that he hadn't heard from in twenty years."

Because the idler has time to ponder, small doings are as interesting as big. Rarely does an essayist notice historical events.

Little things make my days enjoyable. In October the university interviewed candidates for a deanship. I ate lunch with one of the candidates. "Are you from the athletic department?" a waiter asked when we walked into the restaurant. I said we were from the English department, and the waiter led us to a table crammed into a dark corner. "You should have jumped up and pretended to do a slam dunk," Josh said. "Then no matter if you were monsters, gubber-tushed with black teeth, your ankles hanging over your shoes, and your feet stinking and breeding lice, you would have frolicked under the chandelier, swilled champagne and munched pigeon tits soaked in asses' milk, pickled cranes, lampreys stuffed with parsnips, marinated gooseturds, bulls' pizzles bathed in rose water then ground with pomegranates and baked in the shells of chambered nautiluses—in short you would have feasted on the whole ball of cerumen."

Almost as satisfying as Josh's words was my appearance on a radio show. The occasion was the publication of *Walkabout Year,* a book describing twelve months my family and I spent in Western Australia. Listeners telephoned the station to talk to me. Their interests, I quickly discovered, were political, not literary. Sitting in the study, telephone in hand, I listened to the advertisements at the beginning of the program. The first advertisement trumpeted the virtues of a compact disc containing patriotic songs, "all-American songs," the announcer said. The second advertisement praised a book that taught policemen their constitutional rights. The first caller asked me whom I was going to vote for in the presidential election. "Bill Clinton," I said. "A man who can keep himself out of war just might be able to keep this country at peace." The remark awoke every ninny in the nation. For an hour peevish patriots lectured me, preaching that the "country needed Jesus in the White House" and explaining that because constitutional rights were being trampled, the citizenry had to arm itself with Uzis and AK-47s. For a time I was polite, even deferential. Many callers sounded old, and as a child, I had been taught to treat elders with respect. After a while, however, the braying of aged jackasses irritated me. I realized that I was not young. Not my elders but dumbbells my age were scolding me. Suddenly I began to enjoy the program. "Eat a bowl of All-Bran, and clean out your brain," I advised an armament specialist. "You are wandering in your mind," I told another madman, "but don't worry; you can't go far."

My days resemble paragraphs without topic sentences. Beginnings and endings are arbitrary, and thoughts dangle like participial phrases. The sentence that begins the morning simple becomes compound by afternoon and loses its subject by evening. One day I drove to New Haven and ate lunch with Herb and Carolyn Bate. I had not seen Herbie since 1965, when we rowed together at St. Catherine's College in Cambridge, England. Years had treated us kindly, and as I drove back to Storrs, I drifted off onto the slow shoulder of reverie. At Bolton I stopped at Edmondson's farm. Frost had not yet killed the raspberries. "The canes have been picked almost bare," the woman working in the farm store said; "filling half a pint will take a long time." "Time does not matter," I said. Two hours later I had four pints.

"What a surprise," Vicki said, when I handed her the berries. "I didn't know any raspberries were left." "You would be surprised what a person stumbles across when he is not in a hurry," I said. The next day Mrs. Carter, my neighbor, fell on her stairs. I accompanied her to the hospital and stayed while doctors took x-rays of her neck and arm. "This has been a bad day," a teenager sitting on a bed said to me. "Is that so?" I answered. "Yes," she said, "I hit my teacher this morning. Do you think I'll be locked in a cell with padded walls?" "I don't know," I said. When a social worker led the girl into another room, I listened to the conversation of nurses. Two were parents of teenage daughters. "Jennifer has not talked to me in four days," one nurse said. "Sally poured ketchup on the clothes I bought her," another nurse said, then as an afterthought added, "Heinz ketchup from a twenty-eight ounce plastic bottle that I hadn't opened." This fall I spent much time in hospitals. Edward had a minor operation. Before a nurse rolled him into the operating room, an anesthesiologist quizzed me. "Have members of your family ever had strange reactions to anesthesia?" he said. "I am glad you asked," I said. "Anesthesia affects Pickerings in an odd way. Whenever we are given anesthesia, we fall asleep. Isn't that peculiar?" "Very peculiar," the man said, staring at me before writing something on a piece of paper.

The idler rides the local, not the express. When observed from the smoky window of a club car, life intoxicates. Late in October I received a letter from Massachusetts. "Your books," a man wrote, "have given me much pleasure, and I'd like to bring you a present." The present was a hive of honeybees. "Many essayists," the man wrote, "have turned to bugs." Essayists have free time, and they make, he said, "ideal beekeepers." The next day I received a letter from a woman who worked for Carvel. In one of my books I mentioned a Carvel ice cream cake. In December, the woman said, she was sending me a cake, "the sort you like, chocolate in the center, vanilla around the edges." "In your next book," Vicki said, "mention a Mercedes." In the same batch of mail was a letter from a retired doctor in North Carolina. "I thought you would be interested in learning about the doings of one of the characters in *Trespassing*," he explained, mentioning a collection of my essays. "After hearing on the radio that eighty percent of all automobile accidents occurred within twenty-five miles of home, Vester McBee sold her house in Tennessee and moved to Kentucky."

From Nashville my cousin Kathryn wrote. "We are getting ready to move the first of the year," she said, "and I'm not sure

I'm going to make it. We've been in this house for fifty-five years and with everything I discard goes a memory, a few tears, and often a heartache. It's not easy." For me rummaging through house and past is still easy. After I read Kathryn's letter, I explored Eliza's room in hopes of discovering the stuff of future memory. In a drawer I found two poems she wrote last year. "Oh, my, oh, dear, oh, my, / I've something in my eye," the first poem began. "It's big and brown with wings; / It must be one of those four-legged things. / My sense of eyesight is really lost. / I can't even see my fat cat Frost. / But wait. It's flown away. / Yippee, skippee, oh, hooray." Eliza called the second poem "My Journeys." "Dragons and wizards, even a queen, / All of the above I have seen, / On my journeys far and near. / 'Twould take too long to narrate all. / Besides 'tis nearly dark nightfall, / So now I slide into my bed, / While all my words go whirling 'round your head."

On Eliza's bookshelf I found a story entitled, "The Minute Genie." "One rainy day," Louise the narrator recounted, "I went up to our old, old attic to explore because there was nothing else to do and my brother had broken the T.V. As I climbed up the creaky, crooked steps, I saw something out of the corner of my eye. It was a small, black leather case with a strange symbol on it. Carefully I knelt down on the staircase to pick it up. As I grabbed the case my toes got caught in a mousetrap, Master Trapper to be exact. 'Youch,' I cried, tumbling back down the staircase. 'Are you all right, Louise?' called my mother. While extracting my delicate toes from the Master Trapper, I replied in a shaky voice that I hadn't been eaten by a dragon or carried off by a witch, so everything was all right.

"I was about to limp to the bathroom to get some antiseptic for my foot," Louise continued, "when the thought crossed my mind that the case might hold something important. I raced back upstairs and grabbed the case. With an almost superhuman effort I pried open the lock and lifted the top. To my surprise a shimmering mist rose slowly from the case. With a jolt I realized that the mist was coming from a small, smelly, goose-poop green ring. I was disappointed, and I spun around to go downstairs, but then right under my nose, I noticed a minute genie.

"When the genie bowed and squeaked, 'your wish is my command,'" Louise knew what to do, explaining that she had watched tons of movies with genies in them. "'Okay, genie,' I said, 'my first wish is to have a four room library containing books from all the authors in the world.' 'I'm sorry,' said the genie; 'you can either have four rooms, one library, or all the authors in the world. But you cannot have all three.'" Disappointed, Louise fumed, but she tried again, this time wishing for a cocker spaniel.

"Instantly, there was a blinding flash of light, and right under my nose appeared a beautiful spaniel. I should have been pleased, but I was in a fussy mood, and everything irritated me. 'It's not a girl,' I complained; 'I want a girl.' The genie clapped his hands, and the boy dog changed into a girl dog. Still, I wasn't satisfied. 'Its tail is too long!' I yelled; 'its tail is too long!' The genie grumbled something under his breath and suddenly the dog's tail was shorter. 'Good-bye,' said the genie. 'I've never met a more unpleasant master.' And with a frown the genie disappeared." "My dog is whining now," Louise said, concluding the story, "so I'll have to stop talking. I've never had a worst dog."

Louise's day lifted my spirits. For the idler a child's story can transform thought as magically as hocus-pocus. No longer do I read with purpose. Instead I drift through books, most recently the Charlie Bradshaw mysteries, set in Saratoga by Stephen Dobyns, and last night W. H. Hudson's *Afoot in England* (1902). Even the chapter titles were relaxing: "Branscombe," "By Swallowfield," "Whitesheet Hill," "Abbotsbury," and "A Cold Day at Silchester." Hudson called one chapter "An Old Road Leading

Nowhere." Essayists, at least those who have turned to bugs, spend days on old roads and visit all sorts of pleasant Nowheres. This October I ambled into Halloween. My friend George attended a Halloween party dressed as a Catholic schoolgirl. From the Salvation Army in Willimantic, he bought a checkered shirt for $3.95 and "for a couple of bucks" a brassiere "with double D cups." George stuffed the brassiere with socks, and his girlfriend Ellen powdered his face and painted his lips red. "What did people think?" I asked George the next morning in the Cup of Sun. "Did anyone chase you around?" "Chase me? No!" George exclaimed. "Everybody thought I was a Scotsman."

At night I suppose there's not much difference between a Scotsman and a schoolgirl. To prevent such a misunderstanding, though, I wore my costume during the day. For $1.25 at the university bookstore, I bought a pair of "Creepy Creatures Teeth." The teeth resembled rubber dentures and slipped over my gums, infecting me with hoof and mouth disease. My mouth was an orthodontist's dream. Teeth jutted out of red pits like beams. Over my eyes I hung a pair of "Magic Glasses" with thick lenses that made me resemble a nutty bookworm. I topped off the costume with a gray wig. Hair hung over my shoulders in greasy snarls. At nine o'clock Halloween morning I went to the office of a local dentist. Before going in, I looked through the window. The drawing room, as Josh calls the waiting area at a dentist's office, was full of glum patients. I fluffed my hair, smacked my dentures together to start saliva flowing, and burst into the office. "Emergency, emergency!" I shouted, opening my mouth and pointing to my teeth with my right index finger. "Oh, Lord," the secretary said jumping up and clasping her hand over her mouth before disappearing down a hall. "Uhhh," I moaned and stared glassy-eyed around the room. Thoughts of molar and bicuspid vanished from people's minds. When I retire from teaching, I may take up witch-doctoring. Looking at me cured one man's toothache. He bounced to his feet and turned toward the door, resembling a horse ready to bolt through the starting gate. I am an old stager, however, and a step in his direction combined with a grunt settled him back in the chair.

Although the man became a nonstarter, I wasn't ready to scratch Halloween off the calendar. From the dentist's office I went to the university and idled the morning away roaming the campus. I visited the English department, library, bookstore, and the administration building. A candidate for the deanship entered the administration building at the same time I arrived. This time I was not mistaken for a member of the athletic department, and when I bounded into the building, a secretary hurried the candidate into an inner room, shutting the door behind him, "probably locking it, too," Don said. On my hauntings I did not meet anyone in costume. In fact most people refused to look at me, much less acknowledge my groans. "To have acknowledged you," Don said, "would have made people participants in a drama, and we are no longer a nation of participants but observers. Instead of acting, people sit in front of television and live vicariously." "Don is wrong," Josh said; "people don't know who they are today. They are confused about their sexual identities, and the idea of a costume frightens them. They drape themselves in gray behavior and don't dare slip even a foot into the sock of unconventional thought, lest the rest of them be dragged in 'toe-toe' into a terrifying unknown."

Unlike old roads leading Nowhere, manmade roads go somewhere. Only after fifty years of traveling have I concluded that life has no purpose. All significance is artificial, imposed upon existence to reassure the weak. Forcing plan and its companion, rule, upon life confines and narrows. Terrified by vast possibility, man creates educational and religious institutions that pare prodigality down to the acceptable and the approved. Schools teach ways of seeing that blind and methods of defining that obscure. As a result people think and dress conventionally. Last summer Josh was nominated for the presidency of a university. He was interviewed in late October. The day after the interview, Josh came to my office. "No wonder education fails so badly," he said. "People who pretend to manage schools think in platitudes." In the interview Josh was not asked a single thoughtful question. Toward the end of a discussion a vice president for academic affairs asked him, "How do you see yourself in ten years?" "I told the truth," Josh said. "I answered, 'fat, gray, and impotent.'" Alas, the man was so accustomed to answers balmy with soporifics such as duty and commitment he didn't listen carefully to Josh's response and mistook *impotent* for *important*. "Yes," the man said, "our presidents have always been important. We hire people who make a difference."

Not believing that design lies behind life frees me to idle days away on the road to Nowhere. Instead of minding time I lose it. Numbers become toys. One morning I found twenty-nine maggots on my desk. "How did they get there?" Edward asked, wanting an explanation like a good schoolboy. "They crawled out of a walnut I brought home," I said. "Are you sure?" Edward said. "Nope," I said. Every day I spend time standing in front of the sink in the kitchen, looking out the window at the bird feeders in the back yard. "All birds look alike to me," Edward said one afternoon. "Do you ever see anything exciting?" "Yes," I said, "this morning four bluebirds flew into the bittersweet." One day last week I counted twelve gray squirrels under the bird feeders. Among the squirrels was Tiny Tim. In March I saved Tim from George the dachshund. George bit off part of Tim's tail and broke the squirrel's left hind leg. For eleven days I kept Tim in a box and fed him with an eyedropper. After being freed, Tim disappeared, and I suspected a feral cat ate him. Because Tim shuffled when he ran and could not raise his tail off the ground, I recognized him. Although I did not tell Edward, I went outside and called Tim. In truth I went outside three times. Tim always scampered away. Once he perched on a limb and studied me. Something in my voice, I like to think, awakened memory of a simpler time, days before the pursuit of nuts and lady squirrels reduced his life to low purpose.

For a step or two along the old road I imagined other seasons, spring spreading like a green brocade, beyond a fence an apple orchard, blossoms churned creamy by bees, and on the ground bluets dropping through grass like beads of milk. The dream of spring did not last long, however. I have aged and grown so indolent that I am comfortable with season. This fall I spent days traipsing the old road crossing the Ogushwitz meadow. By the end of October goldenrod and milkweed toppled into tangles. Stems of pokeweed bowed out in rickets. Seeds fell from joe-pye weed, leaving sprays of empty receptacles behind. Each receptacle resembled a small white button, and in dark afternoons the buttons glowed, turning the sprays into nibbles of light. Deer beat paths across the meadow. In sunlight the broken stems of goldenrod shined from the paths like damp splinters, shredding up from planks along an abandoned boardwalk. By the beaver pond petaled willow galls resembled black carnations, and male catkins hung from alders in purple clutches.

Early in the morning frost clung to tussock sedge like powdered sugar sprinkled on cupcakes. Sometimes I squatted on my haunches and examined plants. Steeplebush appeared elegant, leaves twisting around stems, their upper surfaces midnight green, their lower surfaces fuzzy and white. Empty seed receptacles resembled minute woven baskets. The baskets were small enough to hold the goals of someone who does not plan life, and

I brought two cuttings home and put them in a tray on my desk. In the tray I also placed a handful of beggar ticks and the seed capsules of white campion. Shaped like urns with ten teeth around their lips, the capsules were smooth and gleamed like butterscotch.

Often I climbed the ridge above the meadow. Along the edge of the meadow curved hedges of barberry and multiflora rose, the canes and sprays of hips on the latter clutching and scratchy. In the woods oak leaves covered the ground like a thick coat. In damp spots ruffles of woodfern decorated the fabric. In places seams split and spotted wintergreen jabbed into sight. Club mosses spread in patches, the creeping stems of running cedar and princess and ground pine resembling loose stitching. Summer's adornments had unraveled, and without their braids of green, trees thinned and shrank into switches. Stone walls tumbled over hills, resembling broken necklaces, the rocks mealy with moss and lichens. Boulders heaved into sight and seeming to shrug, tossed off insubstantial summer, ready to shoulder cold and snow. Thick pipes of poison ivy climbed trees while grape vines knotted saplings into thickets. In the afternoon the sky dulled, and wind coughed across ridges, sounding as if it suffered from the croup. The shell of a chestnut lay across a wall, resembling a galley, beached and long abandoned by vitality. The wood had shrunk into seams. Worms bored dusty holes through the grain, and green and orange fungi shined like flecks of paint. Rain washed down paths, pressing leaves into bales then wedging them between rocks. Liverwort shined atop moss along Kessel Creek, the "leaves" resembling warty green tongues.

I noticed small things, a red squirrel on a stump and then on a grass couch a leaf from a northern red oak, a band of frost wrapping it in white bunting. A procession of Canada geese plodded over the lip of a cornfield. From a distance the birds resembled priests in cassocks, their heads bobbing as they chanted evensong. Below the field the low light of late afternoon shone through a stand of phragmites. The panicles turned silver and resembled ice slivering across a window pane. Often I dallied until late in the evening. Night fell softly like the wing of a huge bird, its black feathers dropping slowly over the hills.

Josh is organized and industrious. He once said dogs should have their tails cut off because the animals wasted energy wagging them. Josh plans days and thinks my meanderings wasteful. "I am not saying you are lazy," he said last spring, "but if digestion required voluntary work, you'd starve to death." "If I were you," I answered, "I would not put my faith in blackberry blossoms." "What?" Josh replied, looking puzzled. "Oh, nothing," I said, drifting onto the old road. "Was it your cousin who sat under the maple tree in his front yard in order to save the shade on the porch?" Josh did not answer. He just strode out of my office, pausing only to shut the door behind him, resembling someone closing the cover of an irritating book.

WIDENESS

"There's a wideness in God's mercy like the wideness of the sea," Frederick Faber wrote in 1852. "If our love were but more simple," the hymn concluded, "we should take him at his word; / And our lives would be all sunshine in the sweetness of the Lord." Much in life blocks sunshine. "Mankind," Josh said recently, "spends most of life in a tomb, rarely glimpsing sweet tolerance or smelling the fragrance of sweeter compassion." For Josh ethnicity is a hard vault. A picture of Serbians near Sarajevo digging up their ancestors was, he told me, "the emblem of our age." No matter where the Serbs go, he said, "they carry with them a past rotten with ancient quarrel and corruption. If man looks at the world through the eye sockets of the dead, he will never see for himself. Ghosts will haunt his days and stand between him and decency. The man who worships bones worships evil." Josh does not saddle rocking horses for debate, but massive Percherons. "Celebration of ethnic diversity in this country sows hatred," he said last week. "Only after people drive ploughs through the past will they be able to see the wideness you write about. Blessed are the orphans, those meek children who have spurned the past and embraced the present, for they are the peacemakers."

Josh enjoys bruising convention. In contrast, most people utter sentiments not their own. Thoughts resemble sound waves. After leaving the mind they bounce off social tuning forks. The forks adjust tone and timbre, after which the thoughts return to the tongue as acceptable platitudes. Occasionally a person tells a discordant truth, and perception unclenches like a fist. Often the person is young, custom and education not yet having taught him to speak harmoniously. Some time ago in Putnam the father of an eighth-grade girl died. The girl loved her father, but when asked about the effect of his death, she told the truth. Instead of hitting the right note by mouthing a conventional answer, she said jarringly, "it embarrasses me."

As people mature not only do they speak conventionally but they live platitudinously. At the middle school in November Eliza played Puck in *A Midsummer Night's Dream.* Two performances were held, one on Friday night, the other on Saturday night. I went to the first performance. Eliza wore blue tights, a silk vest, green shoes with silver bells on the toes, and a headband of red and blue feathers. Two white wings with orange fleur-de-lys in the centers sprouted from her shoulder blades. For me the performance was dreamlike, the evening "over canopied with luscious woodbine, and sweet muskroses, and with eglantine." The second night I intended to stay home. At the university the women's basketball team played. The game was "important, not to be missed," people said, and so I decided, mechanically, to watch the game on television. Just before Eliza's performance, however, I slipped gear. "Basketball games are more common than doctors' cards in funeral homes," I realized. "How often does a father see his daughter play Puck in *A Midsummer Night's Dream?*" I jumped into a suit, and as the curtain rose for the first act, plopped into the seat next to Vicki. I enjoyed the second performance more than the first. When the lights in the auditorium snapped on at the end of the play, I felt like Bottom the weaver waking from enchantment. "I am so glad you came," Eliza said when she saw me. "Did you like the performance?" "Like it?" I said, quoting Bottom; "the eye of man hath not heard, the ear of man hath not seen, man's hand is not able to taste, his tongue to conceive, nor his heart to report, what my dream was."

As a person ages, dreams change. Medical matters narrow vision, and instead of imagining better worlds, one dreams of escaping this world swiftly and so cleanly that family is surprised into mourning. Comments to which I would have paid little attention a decade ago now make me wince. "We've got some real bruisers," a nurse said when I gave blood in September. In December Edward had a small operation. The next week when I took him to the urologist for a follow-up examination, the nurse mistakenly searched for a file on me, not Edward. "Never mind," she said after I told her the appointment was for Edward; "we see everyone eventually." Not all medical commentary makes me hanker for a scrubbed, sterile environment, however. Some remarks appeal to the imagination, dizzying and resembling the wideness of the sea.

The mother of my friend Kate spent much of November in intensive care at a hospital. "Your mother has several problems," the doctor told Kate. The first is her personality, the doctor said, pronouncing her name as if it were a disease. Next, he continued, "she has emphysema and cirrhosis of the liver. Her esophagus has ruptured twice. If it ruptures again, she may bleed to death. The pneumonia and pulmonary embolisms are under control, but blood clots remain in her legs. If she does not drink, the bleeding ulcer will get better." "Is there anything else?" Kate asked when the doctor paused for breath. "Oh, yes," the doctor said, "she is losing her sight, and she is deaf. She suffers from dangerous fibrillations of the heart and then, of course, she has cats." "Four cats," Kate told me, "and two are pregnant." My friend Richard spent Thanksgiving with his ninety-two-year-old father. "I am thankful," Richard's father said at lunch, "that I have not quite gone bananas." The next day Richard drove his father to the cemetery in order to put flowers on the family plot. As they stood looking at the graves, Richard's father turned toward him and asked, "Now, your father, as I recall, is a professor of law. Is he about ready to retire, do you think?"

Ironically, signs of a person's being confined to a narrow life can expand other people's imaginations. Customs that bind members of a culture often startle outsiders. Years ago Josh studied tribes in the Rhodope Mountains in southwest Bulgaria. When a woman's marriage soured, she shifted her wedding ring from the left to the right hand, indicating she had married the wrong man. In the mountains disagreements between families quickly turned into feuds. To prevent quarrels from becoming bloody, women who had recently given birth and who belonged to different families gathered in the local church. Each woman brought her child. On meeting the wife of a member of a family with whom her people had a disagreement, she exchanged babies. After each woman suckled the child from the other family, the quarrel died.

Life sprawls. Uncomfortable with wideness, people order days. They establish institutions, churches and universities, for example, that turn sunshine into shadow and then, standing in the dark, declare the shadow light. People neaten and smooth and in the process imprison themselves. Recently I was in the history department. Taped to a door was a sheet of pink paper. Marching across the paper were five lines of capital letters. "*DO NOT*," the note commanded, "PLACE PAPERS UNDER THE DOOR AS THEY BECOME *FILTHY* AND *DAMAGED*. ALSO, I DO NOT WANT TO SLIP AND FALL AS A RESULT OF STEPPING ON ONE. RATHER, PLACE THEM IN MY MAILBOX IN

THE FACULTY MAILROOM NEXT TO THE ELEVATOR."
"Clearly that man has never filled a tea kettle at a horse trough,"
Josh said after I described the note. "He will come to a bad end,
though he won't be alive to see it."

Amid disorder corruption thrives, and the urge to sweep life
clean so that one does not slip on filth is commonplace. Three
years ago my family and I visited Australia for twelve months.
Several people who live in nursing homes write me. Usually they
send clippings, and just before Christmas when a woman in Indiana received a flyer promoting the Australian lottery, she mailed
it to me, saying, "I hope this awakens good memories." The flyer
originated in Canada. Printed in big green letters across the
middle of the flyer was the statement "I Love To Give Financial
Freedom To My American Friends. . . . Will You Be A Millionaire
In 5 Weeks?" Next to the words was a photograph of a man sitting at a polished desk, a kindly smile laminated on his face, his
hair gray around the edges and neater than papers stuffed into
professors' mailboxes. He held a telephone in his left hand. A
watch with a gleaming leather band circled his right wrist. Above
the watch a half-inch of shirt cuff hung beneath a coat sleeve,
looking as white and clean as a curtain in a hospital room. The
details implied that the man was responsible, and he appeared
to be telephoning a nursing home to break the news that a resident won the lottery, the result of having invested twenty-five
dollars for five weeks of play, easily payable by check, money
order, or charge card: "Visa, American Express, Mastercard, or
Diners Club." "Your Destiny Calls," the flyer stated, "GO FOR
IT! *Order Right Now.*"

The same mail brought a letter to my Uncle Coleman from a
religious entrepreneur. Like the woman in Indiana, Coleman lives
in a nursing home. The man declared that his ministry had long
been "ON THE FRONT LINES FIGHTING FOR GOD AND

COUNTRY!" A crisis had arisen, however. "Now," he wrote, we are "*being threatened by evil world leaders led by the godless, satanic anti-Christ.*" To survive, the ministry needed "A MIRACLE," and the man implored Coleman to "sacrifice" in "the amount of $100 . . . $500 . . . $1,000 . . . $5,000 . . . *OR the best GIFT POSSIBLE. Pray earnestly about it, and God will lead you. You can't outgive God.*" The letters roiled across the day like black clouds, so I left the house and went to the bookstore, searching for bright distraction. "Sam," Sally said, "what's bothering you?" I didn't mention mail. Because preparing for Christmas had tired Vicki, and she was touchy, I said, "the American female gets irritated at Christmas and makes life difficult for others." Sally smiled, then leaned over and whispered, "find a Jewish woman. Christmas won't irritate her." Suddenly sunshine burst through mood, and wide blue opened before me.

Tolerant people appreciate wideness. "That's because many tolerant people don't believe in anything except toleration," Vicki said. "Vicki is wrong," Josh said. "Self-satisfaction is the parent of toleration. Immune to praise or blame, the self-satisfied person is genial. Comfortable with himself, he cares little about opinions. As a result he is a good listener. Distinctions that bring gloom or happiness to others don't touch him. He is the real democrat, at ease with all conditions of men and women. He alone is able to savor wideness without judging or cataloging." Earlier in the week, an acquaintance asked me to write a puff for a manuscript. I instructed her to mail me a five-page sample. The entire book, 385 pages, arrived in the mail. "Seventy-seven times the number of pages you asked for," Vicki said, "and yet you read the whole thing and wrote the puff. God knows what would happen to our savings if some scoundrel tried to sell you chances in the Australian lottery."

Vicki's remark scraped some of the grease off my self-satisfaction. Still, reading the manuscript did not make me withdraw from daily life. Thinking about Faber's wide sea made me mellow. The roar of the ocean smothered clamorous shrillness, and I imagined better worlds. "Put on a sweat shirt with MIRACLES HAPPEN stamped across it," Josh said cynically. Last month Josh saw a mutton-faced woman wearing a shirt that urged people to "Pray for a Miracle." "I will give you a miracle," Josh said to her. "What do you want: to go blind or deaf, to be paralyzed, for your right arm to wither, or for demons to build a subdivision in your womb?" "That's not the kind of miracle I meant," the woman said. "Miracles are not shoes. You can't pick and choose and try them on for size. How about gangrene?" Josh answered. "No," the woman said and hurried away.

Winter is the season of wideness. Leaves tumble from trees like slats broken from fences. After snow falls, light skips across the ground, making night visible. Snow buries walls, and woods open white and inviting. The paths of summer vanish, and walkers stray from the well-trod. During the first heavy snow I roamed fields and ridges for three hours, leaving home at eleven in the evening and returning at two in the morning. Below the sheep barns, snow piled into mounds, resembling bushes blooming cold with white roses. Over lips of boulders snow curled and scurried, the gusts flocks of sanderlings, pattering along a shore then suddenly lifting and circling before dropping back to the sand. Trees clacked and hammered. Over corn fields snow swirled in sheets, rumpling the ground. Gray and blue blossomed in the Ogushwitz meadow, breaking the blanket of snow like shucks, yellow ticking here and there. Overhead, airplanes surfed the sky in constellations. At sunset the next day undersides of clouds glowed burnt-orange like patches of daylilies. The sky turned pale green, and the snow seemed glazed and blue-veined. The moon was full, and when it rose above Horsebarn Hill, it resembled a yellow funnel, the night spilling out like clay over a potter's wheel.

A sinus infection always follows my first winter romp. Three days after the walk, I was sick. Josh visited me. To raise my spirits, he asked riddles, none of which I answered. "Do you know why a hog doesn't fear death?" he asked. "Because after he is killed, he is cured." "Do you know why a man who writes a story appears odd?" he asked next. Since I write books, I thought about the question. Still, the answer eluded me. "Because," Josh said, slapping his right thigh, "his tale comes out of his head." Josh's visit made me better. Although I did not leave the house, I no longer felt confined. I forgot about my aching head and traveled to Carthage, the home of, as Vicki puts it, "a lunatic asylum of characters." Because she is not as satisfied as I am, Vicki judges my friends in Carthage too harshly. When I wander pages in their company, life seems kindly. This fall nothing exciting happened in Carthage. Isom Legg owned a hatchery and for years sold "Legg's Eggs." In October he went to see Dr. Sollows about his tonsils. In the waiting room, Isom read an article on "creative marketing." On returning home, he nailed a sign to the hatchery advertising "Hen Fruits." Isom also started selling rat poison, a combination of lard, alcohol, and phosphorus. When the mixture was heated, the alcohol bound phosphorus to the lard. On cooling, the alcohol separated, and Isom drained it off. Particles of phosphorus stuck to the lard, however. In the dark the phosphorus glowed and attracted rats, especially, Isom explained, "when an icing of sugar sprinkled the lard."

Ben Meadows, Turlow Gutheridge told me, wore a new coat to Enos Mayfield's Inn. Because the coat was expensive and Ben's tobacco crop had failed, Horace Armitage speculated about how Ben got the coat. "Are you insinuating that I stole this coat?" Ben said, sliding off his bar stool. Tall and hard, Ben resembled an elbow of granite, while Horace was soft and pear-shaped. "Calm down Ben," Horace said. "I didn't say you stole the coat. I only said that you bought it without intending to pay for it."

In Gordonsville Hite Flegg killed himself at the end of October. An obituary appeared in the *Carthage Courier.* "I see in the paper," Hoben Donkin said in Ankerrow's Café, "that Hite Flegg committed suicide. He always was one for calling attention to himself. I wonder what he will do next." "He hanged himself on an apple tree," Loppie Groat said, "and what with the kicking and thrashing about, he ruined five or six bushels of apples. What a waste!" Hite was not a great loss. His feet, Slubey Garts said at the funeral, were always wandering into the tent of wickedness.

The big event of the season was the Talent Show at the Male and Female Select School. Around the stage Miss Mabel Campbell, the town librarian, placed "emblems from Shakespeare." Near the footlights lay a red pillow borrowed from Dr. Sollows's waiting room and representing the hump on Richard III's back. Hanging from a hook on the wall was Yorick's skull, made by the shop class at the school for the afflicted in Buffalo Valley. Six feet tall, two feet wide, and covered with crusty yellow scald, the skull startled spectators. Loppie Groat thought it an advertisement for Centaur Liniment, and Hink Ruunt tried to buy it, in order, Turlow Gutheridge reported, to exhibit it as the head of a prehistoric mule. The acts themselves were various. Davy Crockett shot a bear, and Jim Bowie wrestled an alligator. Many people participated. Pocohontas Maintree recited the first lines of "Hiawatha," and Cora Tilly and Juno Feathers sang "Thanatopsis." The musical highlight of the evening was a duet played by Mr. Billy Timmons and Dapper Tuttlebee, Mr. Billy blowing bagpipes, and Dapper plucking the banjo. They opened with "Hog Eye Sally" and closed with "The Old Rugged Cross." During this last tune, the audience stood and sang.

Despite the memorable appearance of Dapper and Mr. Billy,

Turlow Gutheridge stole the show. He appeared as King Bumblebee and told jokes. For his costume Turlow borrowed a striped shirt from Sheriff Baugham, painted a pair of galoshes yellow, and ordered black tights from Nashville. Slubey Garts lent him two church fans for wings, the pictures on both fans the same, Jesus walking across a pasture, a shepherd's crook in his left hand, a lamb under his right, behind him a flock of sheep, all gazing up with doleful, adoring eyes. For a crown Turlow wore mistletoe. Each fall Juno Feathers hung wreaths around the necks of her most prolific sows, and this year she made an extra wreath for Turlow. Although Turlow's jokes smacked of the Ancient of Days, they had not lost savor, and the audience cheered his efforts. "What is the difference," he asked, nodding toward Juno, "between stabbing a man and killing a hog?" "The first," he answered, "is assault with intent to kill while the second is killing with intent to salt." Turlow used props during his performance. "I can spell blind pig with two letters," he said, writing PIG on a blackboard. "Take out the I," he continued, erasing the middle letter, "and the pig is blind." Turlow's most successful joke was Shakespearean. "Two fellows were sitting in front of the courthouse chewing tobacco," he recounted, "when one of them spit, cleared his throat, and turning to his companion, asked, 'Was Rome founded by Romeo?' 'I don't know nothing about that,' the friend responded, 'but I do know Juliet was found dead by Romeo.'" Turlow ended his performance by dancing off stage, singing the old rhyme, "All flesh is grass, and all grass is hay. / We are here tomorrow, and gone today."

The most surprising performance was that of Piety Goforth. In hopes of escaping the clutches of drink, Piety had thrown himself upon the breast of education, taking a correspondence course on writing poetry offered by the University of Tennessee. Piety pulled hard, but the teat, as Hoben Donkin put it, "had run dry by the time it stretched from Knoxville to Carthage." "A crankcase brimming with benzene," Hoben said, "might have made the fires of inspiration leap higher." Still, Carthaginians were generous, and when Piety appeared, they gave him a rousing ovation. The applause touched Piety, and before he recited, he explained the origin of his poem, saying, "The words came to me like the morning sun, and I just opened my mouth like a limpid oyster in the desert." "In a green vale," Piety recited, "shut in by old oak treeses, / Beside a pond where floats the ducks and geeses, / Where cattails and sweet potatoes grows, / And the essence of terrapin greets the nose, / On our rocking chairs we'll pass happy hours. / You'll pick me a yellow bunch of daisy flowers, / And when the starlight beams upon my brow, / I'll squat upon my knees in front of thou. / We'll exhale our love up unto the moon, / And afterwards we'll dine upon champagne and coon."

Everyone in the audience enjoyed the show with the possible exception of Baxley Whicker. From one of the best families in Nashville, Baxley was accustomed to more expensive, if not necessarily more sophisticated, entertainment. Alcohol rather than aesthetics prompted his impatience with the show. Before the performance he refreshed his parched liver at a whiskey ranch, and he arrived at the school primed for a jubilee. His face resembled a pumpkin, one with the candle burning outside the rind rather than inside. Twice Baxley left his seat and tried to catch flies on window panes, but few people in the audience noticed him, as Sheriff Baugham was on stage at the time, doing an imitation of Polly Famous, "the giant, one-eyed waitress at the Odyssey Café." Later Baxley cracked his knuckles, uttered sepulchral groans, and blew his nose with loud trumpetings. Still, people ignored him. The only time anyone noticed Baxley was when Clevanna Farquarhson stepped on stage to recite "The Boy

Stood on the Burning Deck." For the occasion Clevanna wore a long red wig. On seeing Clevanna's hair, Baxley shouted, "Fire!" Even then, the audience thought the cry part of the act, and instead of looking at Baxley, they applauded Clevanna.

Leaving Carthage is difficult. Characters slide papers under doors. I slip on them and tumble out of propriety into broad writing. After the show I returned to Storrs. I had never heard of Centaur Liniment. My house is as cluttered as my essays, and in hopes of discovering a bottle of the liniment, I searched attic and basement. I didn't turn up even a reference to the liniment. A week after coming home, though, I received a package from Miss Mabel Campbell. The package contained *The Centaur Almanac and Cook Book* for the year 1886. While rummaging through the storeroom of the library, Miss Mabel found the *Almanac* in an old desk, and knowing that I was curious about the medicine, she mailed the *Almanac* to me together with another book and a clipping from a newspaper. The paper was tattered and yellow, and the top of the page containing date and place of publication was missing. Miss Mabel thought the paper had been published about the same time as the *Almanac*. Printed on the clipping was a notice announcing the arrival of a doctor in Lebanon, Tennessee, Thaddeus Kirby, "one of those healers who resemble moles," Miss Mabel wrote, "because they can be tracked by the holes they make in the ground." Like Piety, Dr. Kirby suffered from poetic fits, and two lines of medicinal verse appeared at the bottom of the notice. "I can cut a man's leg off—his arm or his head. / I can kill off the living, and raise up the dead."

Measuring five-by-seven-and-a-half-inches, the *Almanac* was thirty-six pages long. Atop the front cover Presidents Grant and Cleveland stared from medallions, both men lumpy and disgruntled. At the bottom of the cover seven cherubs danced through an orange border, the first six naked and the last wearing a dress and holding an umbrella. The cherubs were going to a picnic. The first cherub held a lighted brand over his head while the second carried faggots on his shoulder. The sixth cherub brought the meal, a goose. Before him another cherub carried drink, a big jug wrapped in wicker and probably filled with wine. Spring was in the air as one cherub clanged cymbals and another skipped by tossing seeds over his head. Depicted on the back cover was a statue of "The Diver," a girl in a bathing outfit. The girl's shorts stretched to mid-thigh, and she bent over, her arms an arrow, resembling a child's practicing her first dive. Pharmacists gave the *Almanac* to customers, and stamped beneath the girl was "Compliments of A. D. Champney, Central St., Rockport, Maine. Dealers in Drugs, Medicines and Chemicals, Perfumery, Toilet and Fancy Articles, &c., &c., &c., Prescriptions Carefully Compounded."

The almanac devoted a page to each month of the year. Printed at the top of the page were phases of the moon. The almanac divided the country into regions, and five columns appeared in the middle of each page, detailing times when the sun rose and set for each part of the country. For the first six months of the year the time the moon rose was listed; for the last six months, the almanac listed the time the moon set. Near the end of the almanac appeared six pages of "Cooking Recipes," including, among others, eight soups, ten breads, and seventeen pies and cakes, dishes such as Friday soup and Virginia beaten biscuits. At the end of the almanac was a page of "Hints to Farmers and Housekeepers." To cure earache, readers were instructed to "roast a raisin and bind it on as hot as can be borne." "To remove flesh-worms from the face," the almanac advised, "take a large sized watch key, place the stem directly over the black spot, and press firmly on it." A vehicle for advertising, the almanac urged people to scrub with Zymel cleaner, bathe in Centaur Liniment, and dose themselves with Castoria. In fact, six of the almanac's first ten pages praised the virtues of Samuel Pilcher's Castoria. Under a sketch of a fat, healthy child lying on a pillow appeared a paragraph of grim statistics. "Before they have advanced far in years," the paragraph stated, "most children suffer from some kind of sickness. They cry from pain or languish in stupor. Many of them die before they have hardly begun the journey of life. The bright eyes and rosy lips of every third one are closed by death before their fifth summer has dawned. Twenty-two percent, or nearly one quarter of all children born die before they are one year old; 37 percent, before they are five, and one-half before they are fifteen!" Following descriptions of ventilation and proper food appeared "THE REMEDY." "The true remedy" was "prevention, not medicine, but where errors have occurred we must correct them as far as we can." For two pages of ailments the best correction was Castoria. Signs of thrush, the almanac warned, were "white pimples on lips, in mouth and throat extended to the intestinal canal of infant and nipples of nursing mother. Use plenty of pure soap and water, plain diet, borax wash and gargle and a little Castoria." Scattered amid diseases were rhymes, most composed by amateur poetasters, not quite up to Piety's professionalism. "Bob and Cousin Sue crept down the lane," one rhyme recounted, "Tempting harvest apples for to steal— / That night they yelled with stomach pain / And threw up half their stolen meal. / Next day the doctor was by Bob's side— / But Castoria was given Sue;— / Alas poor Bob, he quickly died / And well, by his grave, wept Cousin Sue." A chorus of inspirational testimonials accompanied the poetry. "If you could hear Kentucky women praise CASTORIA," Green V. Holland wrote from Clover Bottom, Kentucky, "it would do your heart good. No more Castor Oil or Soothing Syrup for our babies."

The almanac devoted three pages to Centaur Liniment, "*the*

most *Powerful, Penetrating, Pain-Relieving Remedy known to Man.*"
Across the first page galloped a bearded centaur, a bottle of liniment high in his left hand, the index finger of his right hand
pointing toward the bottle. Behind the centaur's back streamed a
cape, implying that the centaur was rushing to relieve the pains
of a woebegone rheumatic. Of course, the centaur may have worn
a cape for the sake of propriety. Unlike the cherubs, who were
sexless, the centaur was male. For him to appear in public without clothes would have been rude, no matter his errand. In contrast to trousers, which would have shortened his stride and
galled his legs, making him a candidate for his own medicine,
the cape did not slow the centaur. "The *scarred,* the *lame,* the
crippled, and the *pain-stricken,* seen upon every side of us, show
that although *Remedies are Many, Cures are Few,*" the advertisement began; "here is a preparation which has stood the test of
time, which is an almost *instantaneous* pain-relieving power, has
found lodgment around the earth, and the popularity of which
like that of the fabled Centaurs of old, becomes brighter with
age and better with acquaintance."

The *Almanac* celebrated the global popularity of the liniment.
Sketches of six people from different countries appeared on one
page of the almanac, all of them grasping bottles of Centaur Liniment. While Uncle Sam was tall and straight, John Bull was pudgy
and resembled an Uncle Toby mug. A Turk sat crosslegged, ig-
noring a hookah smoking beside him, his attention focused on a
bottle of Centaur Liniment. Accompanying the sketches were lists
of ailments cured by the liniment. "*The Arabs* and *Egyptians* use
Centaur Liniment for *Scrofula,* Leprosy and Wounds, and *Galls,
Strains, Spavin* and *poisonous bites* upon *horses* and *camels.*" Because Americans had long been familiar with the medicine, the
list of ailments they treated was long. "*Americans* use *Centaur
Liniment* for Boils, Bruises, Burns, Chilblains, Cuts, Earache,

Felon, Itch, Lumbago, Mumps, Neuralgia, *Pain in Back,* Pimples, Poisonous Bites, Rash, *Rheumatism,* Salt Rheum, Scurvy, *Scalds,* Sciatica, Stiff Joints, *Strains,* and Swellings, also for *Sprains,* Kicks, Gall, *Spavin,* and Scratches upon Horses."

Testimonials to the efficacy of the liniment were remarkable. After using the liniment, a resident of Belfair Court House, Virginia, "*Threw away His Crutches.*" When Centaur Liniment cured Riley Hance of ten years of Rheumatism, during the last six of which he was "entirely helpless" and could "hardly move," he immediately visited Leonidas McQuown, a justice of the peace in West Windsor, Michigan, and recorded an "official account" describing the miraculous cure. Two elephants owned by P. T. Barnum ambled across a page. Beneath them was a letter written by Barnum and posted from 438 Fifth Avenue. "Among my vast troop of teamsters, equestrians, horses, camels and elephants, there are always some lame, wounded, galled and strained. My doctors and veterinarians all assure me that nothing has proven so prompt and efficacious a remedy for men and animals as *Centaur Liniment.* If you could supply me a live Centaur, I will give you my check for $100,000."

The almanac praised Zymel, "The Magic Clothes Cleaner." Since I rarely notice dirt, I rushed through the advertisement, pausing only to read a couplet. "Like spots on the sun shone the coat of young Bell, / They vanished like dew after using Zymel." The only other advertisement that interested me was for Wei De Meyer's Catarrh Cure, "the Most Important Discovery for the Relief of Human Suffering since Vaccination." My sinus infection had returned. Antibiotics having failed me, I was willing to read about cures, if not take them. "*More than 200,000 Persons,*" the almanac stated, had "been permanently cured of Catarrh during the past year" by Wei De Meyer's Cure. From Minnesota came testimonials from seven people, "*The Seven Apostles of Min-*

neapolis," one of whom had endured catarrh for fifteen years. A "U.S. Government Inspector" in Brooklyn declared that until he used "Wei De Meyer's wonderful discovery" he had spent four years suffering from catarrh, losing both taste and smell. The "virus *ate through*" his left nostril to his cheek. Not only was his health undermined, but his voice was affected and he couldn't breathe through his nose. "My breath," he recounted, "was terribly offensive, and I felt myself *an object of loathing and disgust.*"

The letter made me queasy, and for a moment I pushed concern for sinuses out of mind. I remembered something Turlow Gutheridge told me during my visit. Two years ago several families seceded from Slubey Garts's Tabernacle of Love and formed the Church of the Chastening Rod. In August the congregation accused Slubey of planting watermelons atop graves in the Pillow of Heaven Cemetery. He did it, they claimed, in order to save money on fertilizer. Watermelons were growing on a couple of graves, but these, Turlow reckoned, sprouted from seeds spit out by initiates of lodges during mystical ceremonies, most probably, Turlow said, the Masons or the Chamber of Commerce.

Turlow's account made me feel healthy, and so I read Wei De Meyer's "Symptoms of Catarrh." Symptoms were divided into six batches or stages. In the first were "Snuffling, Sneezing, Watery Eyes, Disgusting Expectorations, with Intermittent pains, by the side of the nose, back of head, and over eyes." In the second batch the "Head seems to crackle and spin; hearing suddenly ceases upon blowing the nose; buzzing noises and spurts of thin mucous upon the tonsils, or from the nostrils." "Taste, Smell and Hearing Impaired; stopping of one nostril; hawking greenish mucous; dry scales in mouth" marked the third stage. When catarrh spread to the fourth stage a person's nostrils closed, and he swallowed "virulent poison while asleep." "Foetid and Sickening breath" marked the fifth stage, along with "watery stars floating before the eyes" and "watery discharge from genitals." At the discharge I closed the almanac. Flesh may be grass, but I don't enjoy descriptions of mowing.

Along with the almanac Miss Mabel sent *Inquire Within For Anything You Want To Know or Over Three Thousand Seven Hundred Facts Worth Knowing,* published by Dick and Fitzgerald in New York in 1856. Opposite the title page someone wrote a quatrain. Ink had faded, but the words were clear. "If wisdom's ways you wisely seek, / Five things observe with care; / Of whom you speak, to whom you speak, / and how and when, and where."

Four hundred and thirty-four pages long, two columns to a page, fifty-three lines to a column, *Inquire Within* was a miscellany containing discussions of 3,779 subjects. While many discussions were no longer than a paragraph, others stretched through pages. For the satisfied person most things are interesting, and I rummaged through the book, sampling recipes for calf's head pie, both turnip and parsnip wine, and for baldness, a wash made from boxwood leaves. The book contained a column of anagrams, my favorites being *astronomers,* the source of *no more stars,* and *Presbyterians,* which became *best in prayer.* Charades were popular, and the book listed 849 words "which may be converted into ACTING OR WRITTEN CHARADES." I paused over numbers and lists, mulling the fact that the word *and* appeared in the bible 46,227 times. "The difference between rising every morning at six and at eight in the course of forty years," EARLY RISING stated, "amounts to 29,200 hours or three years one hundred and twenty one days and sixteen hours which are equal to eight hours a day for exactly ten years. So that rising at six will be the same as if ten years of life (a weighty consideration) were added, wherein we may command eight hours every day for the cultivation of our minds and the dispatch of business."

I read *Inquire Within* in bed at night. Unlike the early riser who gained days, reading made me lose hours. Usually I fall asleep at eleven o'clock. I read *Inquire Within* for seven nights, on four of which, so far as I can tell, I fell asleep at 10:15. On the other three nights I lasted until 10:30. As a result I lost four hours and thirty minutes during the week. If I subjected myself to a regimen of similar reading, I would lose 234 hours a year during a 365-day year or approximately nine thousand three hundred and sixty hours over forty years, or 390 twenty-four hour days, or 1,170 eight-hour days, this last equivalent to 3.205479 years of eight-hour days. Before resting my head on the bosom of Morpheus, I noticed one or two other things that made me raise an eyelid. The "most proper time" to evacuate the bowels was, I read, "in a morning after breakfast." Leaves from beech trees made good stuffing for beds for the poor. The leaves "should be gathered on a dry day in the autumn and perfectly dried," *Inquire Within* instructed, adding, "it is said that they smell grateful, and will not harbor vermin. They are also very springy."

I was not certain how a leaf could smell grateful. To quibble over such a matter would have exposed me as a pedant, something the book warned against. "Some men," the book noted, "have a mania for Greek and Latin quotations; this is peculiarly to be avoided. It is like pulling up the stones from a tomb wherewith to kill the living. Nothing is more wearisome than pedantry." Not all advice spooned out by the book was salubrious. "Abjure punning. Gentlemen never pun," the book warned, condemning punning as "incompatible with good manners" and damning it as "the wit of fools." Such advice clogs the jocular vein and causes narrowness of sight and soul. For my part I prefer the eye-popping advice given by Loppie Groat to Googoo Hooberry. Googoo had to attend Hite's funeral. Needing a new suit, he consulted Loppie. "Buy something modest," Loppie suggested, "a plain red or yellow suit." How sad it would be not to enjoy the buzzing of King Bumblebee. "What fruit grows on utility poles?" the King asked during the talent show. "Electric currants," he answered when the audience looked puzzled.

After the entry on punning, I read HOW TO WIN A SWEET-HEART. The essay was thorough, taking the emotional and intellectual pulses of several types of sweethearts and then prescribing tonics guaranteed to soothe heartburn. "If approbativeness predominate and causality be moderate," one cure-all began, "you may *flatter,* and if the brain be rather small, put it on *thickly.* Praise their dress, features, appearance, on particular occasions, and any and everything they take pride in. Take much *notice* of them, and keep occasionally saying something to tickle their vanity; for this organization will bear all the soft soap you can administer. When you have gained this organ, you have got the bell-sheep, which all the other faculties will blindly follow on the run." "Now that," I thought, "is real advice," the word *bell* ringing, however, and making me sleepy. I closed the book. Soon I was wandering a midwinter night's dream, the landscape not honeycombed by catarrh, a place where signs invited and never warned "Do Not," where people forgot the past, where the sun was forever golden and the snow rolled mercifully like the sea.

WORDS

"Words," Josh said, "will pay for most things." Years ago Josh's brother Shelby, an elementary school teacher, married a girl from Chappaqua, New York. The girl's father was a banker and sometime art collector. "Shelby," the man said at the wedding reception, dropping an arm smoothly over the shoulders of Josh's brother and steering him like a yacht into the living room; "recently a couple of my investments have addled, making it impossible for me to give you and Harriet a nest egg." "But," he continued, gesturing toward a painting on the wall, "this is Harriet's Chagall. Anytime she wants the painting, she can take it home and do with it as she pleases. Hang it in the living room or sell it, I don't care." When his father-in-law stopped speaking, Shelby thanked him for his generosity. "It's nothing," the man beamed. "If you ever need help with financial matters, call on me." Six weeks later Shelby and Harriet visited her parents in Chappaqua. The Chagall was no longer on the wall. Harriet's father had sold it and pocketed the money.

Four years later Harriet had a baby. When Harriet took the child to Chappaqua, her father made a show of inviting Shelby into his study for, as he said, "a little man-to-man talk." "Shelby," he said, sitting down behind his desk, "I know schoolteachers do not earn large salaries. The baby will strain your finances, and so I have decided to give you a thousand dollars a month until this child and any other offspring you and Harriet may be blessed with are grown." When Shelby visited Chappaqua, Harriet's father always baked wind pudding. Not only had Shelby come to recognize the aroma of empty sound, but he had learned to respond fulsomely. On this occasion, however, the fragrance stuck in Shelby's craw. Instead of acting as his father-in-law expected, thanking him but turning down the gift, Shelby accepted the money. "How wonderful!" Shelby exclaimed. "I can only genuflect before such largesse." "But don't," he continued, his father-in-law looking as if he had walked into an uppercut, "send the checks to me. Send them to Harriet. She has nothing of her own and receiving a present from you would do wonders for her." Before his father-in-law could answer, Shelby stood and walked toward the door of the study. Before stepping out of the room, he turned back toward the desk and said, "Your thoughtfulness leaves me almost speechless. How loved Harriet will feel!" Later that afternoon when Harriet asked Shelby what he and her father discussed in the study, Shelby said, "Books. In the *Times* your father read reviews of the autobiographies of two teachers. He wanted to buy them for me. Unfortunately, I'd already read them. Still," Shelby said, taking Harriet's hand, "the thought was generous, so like him."

"Eighteen years have passed," Josh told me, "and Harriet hasn't received a check." According to Cree legend, words that did not lead to deeds gave birth to the snow snake. The snake lived in an icy cavern, resembling a mouth. Because its fangs were icicles, the snake was a constrictor, luring people into its lair with steamy words. Once a person entered the cavern, the snake coiled around his chest and froze his heart. "How Shelby has endured twenty-two years of talk without becoming cynical is beyond understanding," Josh said. "When I ask about Chappaqua, he describes his most recent visit. Never does he give me a chance to make a venomous remark. He always says, 'and that's the end of my tale,' as the tadpole said when he turned into a bullfrog."

In part Shelby may not react to his father-in-law's words because he no longer hears them. The rational man learns to shut ears as well as eyes. Despite columns of newsprint devoted to their antics, almost nothing that a politician or an athlete says, or does, matters. Moreover, many things differ greatly from the words that describe them. Recently I received a letter from the University of Iowa. Stamped on the front of the envelope was "IMPORTANT TAX DOCUMENT ENCLOSED." Inside the envelope was a note stating that the royalties earned by one of my books had been reported to the Internal Revenue Service, all $17.18 worth, not a matter of fiscal importance. Of course using words skillfully enables a person to steer through the inconsistencies of living. Whenever Carthaginians urged Hink Ruunt to attend church regularly, Hink said he believed in predestination, nailing the conversation flat with, "what will be will be, no matter the time spent in a pew." This past year Hink traveled to Cookeville to buy a Hereford bull. Supposedly a band of robbers was hiding in Chestnut Mound near the road to Cookeville. Before leaving Carthage, Hink bought a pistol. "Hink," Proverbs Goforth asked, "why did you buy the gun? If you meet robbers and you are predestined to die, you are a dead man, gun or no gun. What will be will be." "Yes," Hink answered, spinning the chamber of the pistol, "but it could be the robbers' time to die, not mine, and if I'm the Lord's chosen vessel, I want to be prepared to do His will."

"A man," Slubey Garts said, "can spend his life in the field of gospel labor, his soul creaking under hundred weights of good works like a cart loaded with sheaves, but if he does not blow a trumpet before himself, only God will notice." Like potions of Easy Life Powder sold by faith doctors, words are cheap. Flattery enchants, and a teaspoon doled out here and there keeps palms oily and does more for reputation than years of charitable action. "His talk is so melodious that dead folks sit up in coffins and put on hearing aids just to listen to him," Loppie Groat said, describing a sermon preached by Beagon Hackett at the Baptist Church in Carthage. The Baptist Church towered over Main Street, while Slubey Garts's Tabernacle of Love squatted on the low ground above the Cumberland River. In spring the river flooded. "Instead of marching to Zion with the Army of Righteousness," the congregation floated, Turlow Gutheridge said, "becoming the Navy of the Lord." Dampness breeds envy. Despite being an admiral in Jehovah's service, Slubey cast a rancorous eye upward, envying those legions who tramped dryly to Glory, collection plates rattling before them like tambourines. Although Beagon was a fellow member of the Lord's General Staff and recently had fought a good, but losing, fight against a "coven of dark ones" who planned to open a movie theater in Carthage, Slubey did not enjoy hearing his religious ally praised.

"When you find sugar," Slubey said to Loppie Groat, "you'll discover dead ants." On Loppie's looking puzzled, Slubey told an instructive tale. In the hills above Red Boiling Springs, a giant lived in a cave. Handsome, the giant had long golden hair that curled down over his shoulders. The giant's voice was sweeter than honey, and when he spoke, bees flew out of the forest and circled his head, their buzzing sounding like the pantings of a harp. Every so often, though, a hog or a sheep vanished. The citizens of Macon County were tolerant and believed in leaving the giant alone, especially since gossip about him brought a horde of anthropologists to Red Boiling Springs each June. The anthropologists stayed in local hotels and what they spent for room and board more than recompensed for any loss of livestock. Also, a baggage train of ladies followed the anthropologists. The ladies were not Weeping Marys or Cumbering Marthas. Molded from more imperfect clay, they made Red Boiling Springs a lively summer resort. Still, the loss of a prize boar or heifer sometimes upset a farmer, and he decided to settle accounts with the giant. No matter the caliber of their guns, people who sought the giant did not return from the woods. When a farmer appeared at the entrance to his cave, the giant invited him to dinner, talking so kindly that the man always put his gun down. For his guest the giant cooked a fine dinner. The giant did not join the farmer in eating, explaining that a patch of greens he ate recently had proved wormy, making him bilious.

After the meal the giant fetched an ironstone jug of moonshine from a larder in the cave. Next he filled two pipes with dark Virginia tobacco, for himself a pipe as large as a bucket, for his guest a smaller pipe, the bowl carved out of orange amber. The farmer soon became drowsy, the moonshine rising to his brain in a cloud and the tobacco smoke hovering around him like a mist. Eventually the farmer shut his eyes. Never did he open them again in this world. As soon as the farmer's eyelashes brushed his cheekbones, the giant's head spun around. Under the golden hair at the back of his skull lurked a monstrous face. From the forehead glowed a single blood-red eye, while venom dripped from two yellow fangs. Before the farmer could twitch, the giant bit through the man's neck, crushing bones as if they were twigs.

The giant lived for decades. He would probably still be alive, Slubey told Loppie, if he had not dined upon a farmer high in cholesterol. The farmer spent decades grazing in paddocks rich with fried chicken, cheese grits, deviled eggs, green beans piled atop ham hocks, Sally Lunn, sweet potatoes with marshmallows sticking to them like slush, and groaning boards bending under pralines, divinity, and then chess, half-moon, and black bottom pies. The farmer was so fatty that the giant drank four jugs of moonshine with his meal. That night when the giant leaned over to blow out the candle by his bedside, a fog of alcohol escaped from his lungs. The candle ignited the alcohol, and before the giant felt hot, he was incinerated. The pile of ashes was huge. Winds scattered the ashes, blanketing the floor of the cave. The ashes made fine fertilizer, and for years farmers dug them out of the cave and ploughed them into fields. "Agronomists," Slubey concluded, "said the ashes were bat droppings, but folks born in Macon County knew better."

Although words can transform perception, they cannot always influence action. Carthage was dry last summer. When crops began to wilt, Proverbs Goforth asked Slubey if he should pray for rain. "Not yet," Slubey said, glancing out the window, "the wind is not right." Often words fail to shape perception, no matter the plausibility of what they state. Three years ago a handful of parishioners seceded from the Tabernacle of Love and formed the Church of the Chastening Rod. Ever since the secession members of the church have accused Slubey of theological misbehavior. Besides the Tabernacle, Slubey owns a funeral home, a graveyard, and a coffin manufactory. Last summer members of the church started the rumor that Slubey sold secondhand, or preowned, coffins, as a prosperous undertaker in Hartford advertises them today. Like most successful entrepreneurs Slubey had a host of apologists, and the rumor soon vanished in the cistern of time, Pharaoh Parkus declaring, "the translucent stream of the refulgent Son rains upon Slubey like the watery element in a shower bath, cleansing him with the Blood of the Lamb."

Words can be so vital that even misuse quickens life. Zibethum Hooberry was a plumber. Expert at resuscitating both indoor and outdoor arrangements, Zibethum earned a good living. Zibethum was also an amateur linguist, priding himself more on his knowledge of prepositions and conjunctions than he did mazes of P-traps and cleanouts. After work he put on eyeglasses, the lenses of which were bigger than morning glory blossoms, and, he said, "sniffed gingered nosegays, the exhalations of which are so harmonious they darken sunbeams." Zibethum's poetic talk startled and amazed, resembling, Turlow Gutheridge said, "a side show at the Smith County Fair." One day while unplugging a sink in the boys' bathroom at the Male and Female Select School, Zibethum heard seventh graders speaking French. That evening when Loppie Groat visited his house, Zibethum invited him into the parlor and pointing to a chair said, "squatty-vous." Man cannot escape the influence of trade, and Zibethum forever tried to straighten the odd twistings of language, making words flow logically like drain-waste-vent pipes, or the DWV system, as it is known to the plunging brotherhood. Because of gravity, possessives, he thought, should tumble cheek by jowl after *my* and *mine, your* becoming *yourn*; *her, hern*; and *his, hisen*. Like most original thinkers, Zibethum had little use for the academy. Professional linguists, he said, attended a lyceum and as a result did not know their backflows from their soil stacks. "Lyceum," he told Loppie, "is derived from Greek and Latin, the *ly* being Greek for story; the *ceum,* Latin for watch them; the word itself then meaning 'watch them lie.'"

Even when words are used well, people misunderstand one another. According to Scottish story, Adam and Eve spoke Gaelic, while the Archangel Michael spoke English. Because they spoke different languages, a ruinous mistake occurred. God decided to forgive Adam and Eve's eating the apple, and He sent Michael to Eden to inform them. Unfortunately Michael's voice roared like a cataract. Moreover he carried a flaming sword in his right hand as an emblem of justice tempered by mercy. The side of the blade that faced outward burned red-hot, while the underside was cool and blue. Unable to understand English, Adam and Eve misunderstood Michael. His deep voice terrified them, and when flames from the sword flared over their heads, they bolted through the eastern gate of Paradise and like noxious worms burrowed out of sight deep in the Wilderness. For His part God misinterpreted their actions. Thinking they scorned His mercy, He cursed their loins, letting a lazar-house of ailments rain down upon their offspring: spasms, convulsions, epilepsies, fierce catarrhs, moping melancholies, and silent Pestilence swinging a bloody scythe.

Even people who share language interpret words differently. Although only fifty-five miles separate Nashville and Carthage, habits of speech differ. Last month Coker Knox visited Turlow Gutheridge. Turlow introduced Coker to the Pardue brothers, David and Jonathan. The Pardues looked alike, and on meeting them, Coker said, "You must be twins." "No," David replied, shaking his head solemnly, "we are what's left of triplets." In Carthage relationships in families can be as confused as agreement between subject and verb. When he met Zibethum Hooberry, Coker asked if he was "closely related" to Cerumen Hooberry. "No, we have the same mother and father," Zibethum answered, "but we are only distantly related. I was the second child born in the family, and Cerumen was the ninth."

Words can deflate as well as puff. Edward is twelve, and much that I say embarrasses him. Last week I drove his friend Todd home after a basketball game. Edward accompanied us and sat with Todd on the back seat. The Toyota accelerates faster than the Mazda. "This car goes too fast for me," I said applying the breaks. "Before I know it I'm going forty miles an hour." "Edward was so ashamed of you last night," Vicki said the next morning. "He said that seventy or eighty miles an hour would be fast, but forty is 'really stupid.' The next time you drive him and a friend, he doesn't want you to talk." Except when one's children make up the audience, talk usually embarrasses speakers, not listeners. For my class last week students read a story in which manners were important. I explained that civility made social life possible. When a person met someone and said, "How do you do," I cited as an example, he did not expect an answer bulging with intimate detail. He merely expected the person to reply innocuously and conventionally, saying something like, "I'm fine. How are you?" The man would be startled if the person he met said, "Oh, it's so good of you to ask. I'm suffering from slow movement of the bowels. But I took a dose of Metamucil before breakfast, and soon I expect my difficulties to pass." Unfortunately, I misspoke myself and said, "Oh, it's so good of you to ask. I'm suffering from slow movement of the balls."

Early in February, Vicki and I attended a production of *La Traviata* at the university. Before the opera Vicki and I ate supper in an art gallery. We sat at a round table with seven strangers. Across from me was the new head of the French department. The woman appeared to be forty-five years old. On her left sat her companion, an older man, almost seventy with a cherubic, retired expression on his face. The woman was not wearing a wedding ring and was so attentive to the man that she seemed daughterly, or so I assumed. "And this is your father?" I said nodding toward the man. "Is he visiting you especially for *La Traviata*?" "Not father," the woman replied curtly. "He's my partner." The words jarred me, not nearly so violently, however, as the kick Vicki delivered to my ankle. If dinner had been a football game, the waiter would have penalized Vicki fifteen yards for unnecessary roughness.

I am a callused conversationalist, however, and embarrassment does not bruise my mind. Pain is a different, more substantial matter, and the throbbing in my ankle did not vanish until

Alfredo's drinking song in the first act. Words not understood sometimes have more power than words understood. *La Traviata* was sung in Italian, and I was not able to dissect songs and pick out the intricacies of language and plot. Instead, as the music billowed, I floated through the evening, buoyed up by currents of association. Act II was Father's favorite act in opera. As the songs swept into the auditorium—"Pura siccome un angelo," "Dite alla giovine," and "Di Provenza il mar, il suol chi dal cor ti cancellò"—I roamed the past, not Provence's sea and soil but Tennessee and Virginia. Years slipped away, and I visited Mother and Father. We did not talk much because music erases both time and words. Still, when the opera ended, I did not want to leave the auditorium and push out into the nagging, noisy present.

Because so many words rub against a person during a day, literature may have lost its capacity to move people as much as other forms of art. This past summer in Carthage the Chamber of Commerce sponsored a crafts fair. The Hall of Canvases was the highlight of the fair. Long after the fair closed, the Hall clung to mind like dollops of oil paint on a palette, flowing and spreading as thoughts brushed through them. Several pictures puzzled viewers. LaBelle Watrous painted a green nanny goat suckling a red grasshopper. A sleeping giant stretched across another canvas. A crooked woman wearing seashells stood beside the giant's right foot, leaning on a saw. The woman had cut off the giant's big toes. Not blood but people streamed out of the wounds, all wearing white and carrying black candles. The painting was submitted anonymously, probably by someone from Red Boiling Springs, Slubey Garts said. "People there think more about giants than we do in Carthage. We're just a simple flock of peckerwoods and poor, bedraggled sinners."

Not all the exhibits were mysterious. Turlow Gutheridge painted a picture of Battery Hill in winter. Cedar trees pushed through snow like exclamation marks. "Turlow paints so well," Loppie Groat said, "that I shivered every time I looked at the picture. I knew the picture would give me a chill, so I wore a sweater and mittens the second time I went to the fair." Juno Feathers painted two hogs breaking into a chicken house. "Those pigs were so fat that I could smell bacon sizzling," Zibethum Hooberry said, smacking his chops.

La Traviata provided only a brief respite from words. Last week my friend Raymond said the subject of my essays was words, "not ideas or places or even family, but words." In truth there are moments when lives I scratch across pages seem more vital than the one I live hour to hour. In bed at night I rarely think about the class I will teach at eight o'clock the next morning. Instead I marvel at the doings of the Hooberrys. Just last week Beagon Hackett congratulated Zaidee Hooberry on reaching her ninety-sixth birthday. "What has enabled you to become an old Soldier of the Cross? When others have tumbled from the walls of Zion, what has sustained you and been an unfailing source of comfort?" Beagon asked, pressing a Bible to his bosom and expecting an inspirational answer. "Victuals and tobacco," Zaidee said, fixing Beagon with a wayward eye before adding, "then when I'm feeling poorly, dandelion wine."

In my house melody does not weave eloquently through days. Instead words clatter cacophonously. Like refrains the children bang sentences about, often repeating variations of what I say. "You have a lot of writer friends," Edward said to me last Thursday at dinner. "Do you have any wronger friends?" "That's classic Dad," Edward said proudly a moment later. Last month Eliza wrote a story entitled, "Why the Horned Owl Calls 'Who.'" "A long time ago," she began, "when the world was young," the animals misbehaved, and God decided they needed "a firm hand to govern them." Because He was in heaven, God could not discipline the animals Himself, so on the banks of the Celestial River He "fashioned a chief for the animals out of mud." On top of the chief's head He set horns "as a symbol of superiority." "God called the creature Owl."

Although wise, Owl was vain and overbearing. He soon became a nuisance, and the other creatures "were very annoyed with God for making him." When Owl ordered woodpeckers to construct a suburb of tree houses, elders in the animal community scheduled a town meeting. The meeting was held at noon when Owl was asleep. Initially, the meeting seemed doomed to ineffectuality as the animals complained about Owl's behavior without suggesting how to change it. Finally, though, Badger spoke. "Without his horns," Badger said, "Owl is nothing." Unfortunately no one "had any notion how to separate Owl from the horns," and the meeting ended indecisively. While flying home, though, Swallow decided to look in on Owl. On arriving at his tree, she discovered him "sleeping soundly as a fledgling." Swallow seized the opportunity to distinguish herself and, creeping into his hole, started pecking Owl's horns. After she pecked for two hours, the horns fell off. Swallow was a kindly bird, however, and thinking Owl looked drab, she "pulled out two of her pinfeathers and stuck them where Owl's magnificent horns used to be." Swallow then flew away, "lugging the horns with her." She dropped them into the middle of a lake where they sank and "became part of a merman's castle." In the meantime "the first rays of moonlight woke Owl, and he flew to a pond to wash his feathers and admire his reflection." "But what did he see in the water? No mighty horns but ridiculous feathers standing where his pride and joy once loomed!" Owl then hurried back to his tree where he sulked, "inconsolable." When he finally left the tree, he avoided other creatures. Instead, he wandered the world asking, "Who, who took my horns?"

The night before Valentine's Day I had a salacious dream. Nymphs cavorted across a lawn then posed, assuming postures vaguely resembling Greek statues. Although the marble ladies encouraged me to misbehave, I declined. When I woke on Valentine's Day, I was disgruntled. On marrying Vicki I forswore antics of the sort the nymphs suggested. Still, sporting about in the unconscious isn't the same as philandering around town. As I sat on the edge of the bed, pulling up my socks, I regretted becoming so upright that I resisted temptation even in a dream. "Don't worry," Vicki said, "you acted in character. For you misbehavior has always been wordy not fleshly." Years ago I read an essay in which a psychologist discussed men who confused "the penis and the pen." Only in a dream could such confusion arise. Waking would, in any case, erase all grammatical errors. Be that as it may, however, only pens have blotted my copybook. Still, like hormones words occasionally make me stray from line and rule. In late January the Friends of the Mansfield Library sponsored their annual book sale. Residents both donated and bought books, and proceeds from the sale supported purchases for the library. I donated forty books to the sale. Good books delight and intrigue. Unfortunately some of the books I took to the sale were coldly cerebral. In hopes of making them more attractive, I inscribed the books warmly. "To Achilles," I wrote on the title page of one book, "In memory of the night we spent together at the bathhouse. You have my word Clara will never know. Love, Patroclus, your own little coochie-coo." "Blithe," I wrote in another book, "Can you believe that twenty years have passed since the seventies? You and I both have families. But sometimes I wonder what happened to our love-child. She is now almost grown. How foolish and young, yet how loving we were. Your Spotty."

The inscriptions resembled bits of story. For a moment I was tempted to use common names. But I worried that someone might recognize a mate, and one of my fragments might become the first paragraph of a mystery entitled *Murder after the Book Sale*. One mischievous sentence usually runs on into another. The next day Francis received an advertisement in the mail, offering him the opportunity to subscribe to *Playboy*. When awake, I resemble the straightlaced me of dreams. On the front of the advertisement were women resembling freshened Guernseys, udders hanging down to their hocks. The advertisement was mailed from Iowa, so I wrote a letter sour with the milk of human irritation to the attorney general of the state. I began the letter by noting that the advertisement had been sent from Harlan, Iowa, to my fourteen-year-old son. "Take a peek at the world's most enticing Playmates in the hottest poses we've ever published," I wrote, quoting the advertisement. "Pleasure has never been this tantalizing, this delicious. Each page sizzles." "For all I know," I said, "every fourteen-year-old in Iowa subscribes to *Playboy,* and every night dines not upon mathematics and literature but upon a sizzling meal of bosom and buttock.

"I showed the advertisement to Josh, a distinguished colleague of mine," I continued. "'I always thought,' I said, 'that Iowa was a wholesome family sort of state.' 'Humbug,' he responded, 'Iowans are about as wholesome as the Crusaders who captured Jerusalem in 1099.' Josh always goes too far, and this particular comment overshoots the mark a bit. But certainly such advertisements do your state little good. At the least they change one's concept of a Hawkeye, the reference shifting from an ornithological to a gynecological vision. From thousands of mailboxes across the nation now rises a picture of herds of young Iowans devoting their energies to scrutinizing the private parts of the human female."

A week after mailing the letter I went for a long walk in the woods, and my bile broke. The world is round, but words are square. Words determine vision. Sentences and paragraphs obstruct the imagination and block thought. As a result people often see words, not the objects they actually observe. In the woods I dreamed of escaping the limitations of meaning, all those words that define and pin people and life to categories like insects mounted in boxes, words that refer to race, for example, words that structure thought and make life mean. Apart from words I imagined blundering into the heart of things, the green of spring or the yellow of fall. As I age, I dream more and more of a silent world. Far above the babel of promises and the hiss of lies and whispers, heaven is wordless. Understanding is intuitive, or so I sometimes imagine. On the other hand, words are the sea on which I have launched an armada of worm-eaten stories. Last month Monroe Dowd appeared before Judge Rutherford, charged with stealing chickens from Juno Feathers. Having seen Juno's painting at the fair, Monroe said that pigs raided the henhouse. "Monroe, you have attended prayer meetings," Judge Rutherford said. "Do you know what will happen to you if you lie?" "I suppose I'll go to hell," Monroe answered. "Good," the judge said, smiling like a Sunday school teacher. "Now what do you think will happen if you tell the truth?" "Well, Judge," Monroe said, rubbing the side of his head with the index and middle fingers of his right hand, "I reckon I will go to jail."

Walks distract and relieve. In the woods Iowa again became a creamy, wholesome place where Guernseys lumbered about on four legs, not two, and milking machines pulled on cows instead of squeezing money out of children. In January bales of snow toppled out of the sky, and shredding filled depressions and caught against windbreaks. When the snow melted, the Fenton River flooded the Ogushwitz meadow. Ice minced the stems of goldenrod, and water swirled the grounds across the meadow.

After the water receded, the mince remained and, freezing, resembled batter stuck to the sides of a mixing bowl. Strewn across the field were slabs of ice, some piled atop each other like buckled sidewalk. Smaller bits stuck out of the ground like trays tossed into a dumpster. Ice puddles glowed like mirrors, their surfaces thin panes of ice. Below the panes were empty spaces, the water under the surface of the puddles having drained away before freezing. Snow cushioned the edge of sound, and when I stepped on the mirrors, they didn't pop so much as ripple into splinters.

Back within its banks the river shuffled along, hunks of ice occasionally scraping banks and sounding like shoes sliding across dance floors. When the weather turned cold again, ice collected around rocks in the river bed and pushed upward through the stream, resembling lumps of waterlogged sugar. Shelves of ice unfolded from banks. Along edges of the shelves water turned in rills, the bows resembling soft flames. Ice dangled from snags and hemlocks. Some icicles resembled fingers, bulbous with knuckles; others stood in ranks like pipes on lutes. From opposite banks tree limbs reached out toward each other like the arms of couples promenading through old-fashioned country dances. Often after a snow I walked beneath hemlocks. The quiet was soft and fleshly. Clumps of snow slid off branches and tumbling onto limbs exploded in mists. When the clumps did not shatter, they fell silently, pocking the surface of the snow when they hit the ground. One afternoon I watched eight deer feeding at the corner of a field. Another day I saw a great horned owl hunched in an oak, its eyes yellow coals, white feathers curving linty beneath his beak. I studied the owl until he lifted himself off the limb and like a small, heavy keg rolled silently away through the trees. Later I heard him calling, his voice an echo bouncing off a thick bluff.

Often I walked through afternoon into night. Some afternoons day sloughed quietly into dark. Other afternoons the sky became a turquoise bowl, here and there amid the glaze bits of silver shining buffed. Sometimes night sank like smoke pressed down over a fire by a damp rag. Wind combed snow off hilltops, and stubble jutted upward. The stubble was oddly comforting, reminding me of syllables, both a remnant of words that had been planted last spring and a harbinger of pages soon to be sowed. Although I often plan to lie fallow, spring pulls words from me. No matter the periods I hammer onto paper, words trail after me, much as Monroe Dowd's sow Sweetbreads once followed him around Carthage.

Last summer Monroe fell in love with Vester McBee. To no avail he sent her baskets of vegetables, country bouquets blossoming with corn, squash, tomatoes, and butter beans. Finally he bought a love potion from Daddy Snakelegs. One day late in August he saw Vester sitting outside the courthouse, eating lunch. The day was hot, and Monroe rushed to Barrow's grocery and bought a cold watermelon. After punching a hole in the rind with an ice pick, he poured the potion into the melon then hurried back to the courthouse and offered Vester a slice. Unfortunately, when Vester was young, she ate a watermelon that grew behind a privy. From the melon she caught typhoid and almost died. As a result she couldn't stand to look at a watermelon, no matter the temperature. The failure of love took Monroe's appetite away. Monroe, however, rarely let anything go to waste, items that belonged to him or items that belonged to others, and so he took the melon home and tossed it into the trough for Sweetbreads.

"From that day on," Turlow Gutheridge told the lunchtime crowd at Ankerrow's Café, "Sweetbreads followed Monroe everywhere. She knocked the railings off the pen and trailed him around town rumbling piteously. She made so much noise that folks could always tell when Monroe was about. For a fortnight chickens led charmed lives. Love and Monroe's business did not make good companions, and after two weeks Monroe sold Sweetbreads to Dinwidder the butcher. The next night foxes or coons or something broke into three chicken coops." Although my words often grunt inconveniently and embarrassingly, I am not ready to parse my love into a freezer of spare ribs, blade steaks, and decorous silence. Yesterday was February 29. Red-winged blackbirds appeared in the backyard for the first time this year. Late this afternoon I am going to wander field and wood in hopes of flushing a flock of seasonal, descriptive words.

HORCHOW GARDEN

The *Horchow Garden* catalog arrived early in February. On the cover English ivy rumpled over a wall, looking like a green cable-knit sweater. A wall hanging swung out from the ivy, resembling a cupboard door. Near the top of the hanging a square window opened onto the wall. A barrette of iron bands cinched the window into panes, and braids of ivy hung over the muntins. From two clay pots buckled to the sill of the door daisy chrysanthemums burst upward, the pots resembling bonnets, the blossoms yellow tatting, stars of doubles and purls. Below the flowers trailed a ruffled fringe of ivy, this time not the dark Woerner cultivar on the wall but Eva, small scalloped gray leaves with a trim of white tacked around the edges.

Strangers think my backyard drab. Iris don't bloom. The woodpile has collapsed, and weigela is dying twig by twig. To me, however, the backyard is a garden, one I force each year after catalogs arrive. Last February imagination transformed my single acre into pastures and hillsides ringing with creeks. Horchow did not advertise many plants, so this year I laid down a brick courtyard, surrounded on three sides by golden limestone walls. Despite the season trumpet vines dangled from stones in orange clutches while canes of winter jasmine swayed yellow with flowers. Clumps of thyme and catmint pushed out from crevices in the wall like embroidered pincushions. Hardiness zones mean little to the imagination, and down the slope west of the terrace, a jacaranda bloomed, its flowers draining together into a mauve pool that sank deep through the blue sky. East of the terrace frangipani blossomed, thin limbs clutching bouquets of creamy white and yellow flowers.

I planned to spend afternoons on the terrace, and so I thumbed the catalog, searching for furniture. I like finials, but the only finial in the catalogue resembled a pineapple. If Horchow grew domestic varieties, watermelon or summer squash, I would have bought a grocery cart full. To a shagbark hickory I nailed a bird house shaped like a ten-gallon hat. The hat cost sixty-five dollars. I hoped bluebirds would fill the crown with fine grasses, but I suspected starlings would stuff it out of blocking with trash. Beside the back door to the house I attached a pair of brass carriage lamps, reproductions of gas wall sconces popular at the end of the nineteenth century. The lamps cost $265 apiece, but later in summer they would attract flurries of moths. Near an end of the wall I hung a gate, although no path was visible. Wrought iron morning glories curled across the gate, leaves and blossoms dangling from rusty tendrils. In imagination gates don't need hinges or latches. Instead they swing open and inviting.

I like planters, and I bought two, each a rusty tin pot nineteen inches in diameter and sitting on an iron stand twenty-seven inches tall. Planters and stands cost $798, and into them I stuffed mounds of lavender: English, Spanish, Provence, and Lavandin. For parties I bought cast aluminum chairs and tables, the basket-weave design turning backs and arms into metal lattices. A dining table and four chairs cost $1,499. In imagination price matters little, and I bought one complete set and two extra chairs at $299 each, then a bench priced at $499. The chairs and tables were heavy and dreary, but the pieces withstood rain and carpenter ants better than wicker. Moreover, their hard bottoms would not mildew like fabrics and cushions. What I really wanted to buy was a settee and armchairs made from teak. The pieces glowed like sweet potatoes. Unfortunately, they were not hardy enough for outdoors, and my imagination wasn't up to building a sunroom in order to accommodate covetousness.

I did not place the furniture carefully. In fact I only unpacked it and told the children to arrange it. Life's little doings kept drawing me away from the terrace. A neighbor went to Hawaii for ten days, and I helped Edward feed her cats. Amid trash in her yard I found a rhododendron that had been chopped out of the ground. The plant was still green. I don't like to see things die, so I planted it behind our house. "Another patient for the plant hospital," Vicki said.

One afternoon I gave blood. Lying on the pallet beside me was a slight man with a goatee. The man looked like a psychologist. While blood boils out of me, I chatter like a kettle on a stove. I asked the man how his corpuscles were gurgling. Instead of answering he clamped his legs together and rolled his head away from me toward the wall. That was a mistake. Josh once told me that psychologists resembled sensitive plants. I decided to test the proposition and see whether the man's veins behaved like leaves on a silk tree. To that end I shot a syringe full of gory anecdotes into the air, tales dripping with needles migrating past biceps into armpits and tubes rupturing like aneurysms, spraying warm blood in sticky gouts. Josh was right. Soon I heard a nurse say to the man, "you have stopped flowing. I will have to reposition the needle."

One day I spoke to a ladies' book club. I signed three books, drank a cup of tea, and ate two Pepperidge Farm cookies, both Milanos. Another day I had an eye examination, my first in eight years. A nurse tested my ability to see color. "Read the number on the page," she instructed, handing me a small book. Patterns of colored dots appeared throughout the book. On the first page an orange five curved like a serpentine wall across a blue lawn. Five was the only number I found in the book. "I have not seen anyone so color blind in years," the nurse said. "Do you really write about nature?" "You bet," I said.

Eliza and Edward played basketball on town teams. Many evenings I drove them to games. While sitting in bleachers, I tried to arrange furniture on the terrace. Doings in games or on walls always distracted me. A banner hung above a stage in the gymnasium of Hall Memorial School in Willington. Green letters as big as stalks of corn declared "You Can't Keep A Good School Down." Ornaments surrounded the letters in tassels, in one or two cases perching on them like smuts. A different child painted each ornament: a basketball with the right side caved in; a computer, the screen black and down; and a palette blooming with pots of paint, blue, yellow, black, and green oozing and clotting. To the left of the *You* stood a falcon, the school mascot, the bird's beak resembling orange shucks and its legs hidden behind purple tights, not feathers. Over the falcon's shoulders draped a purple and white cape, making the bird appear jaunty, "a high-flyer," Vicki said. The game itself was typical. Eliza's team, the Cheetahs, started slowly, falling behind 4-2 at the end of the first quarter, then 10-4 at half-time. At the end of the third quarter the score was 19-4. In the last quarter, Eliza's team "burned the nets," as Vicki put it, and the final score was 21-12. Eliza did not score. In fact she only scored three points in twelve games. "She's our defensive specialist," the coach said.

Vicki's father died in December. He attended Princeton as an undergraduate. Afterward he taught in the English department for thirty years. In March a memorial service was held in his memory in the Princeton Chapel. Vicki asked me to speak, and I spent time in February tidying remarks instead of sitting on the terrace. Vicki's father had a robust sense of humor, and the stories he told about his undergraduate days were merry. When Vicki's father was a senior, a French professor invited him to his house for dinner. The man raised the meal like a well-wrought building, each dish a floor slipping harmoniously atop the previous course. Just before dessert the man excused himself from the table and went into his bedroom. He was gone some time, and Vicki's father assumed he was fetching a tray of liqueurs. Vicki's father was mistaken. As Vicki's father sat back in his chair mulling the delights of Drambuie and Grand Marnier, the professor suddenly appeared in the doorway to the dining room. He was, as the British would put it, completely starkers. "Around the table and through the house he chased me," Vicki's father said. Vicki's father escaped with both honor and sense of humor intact. He said nothing about the evening. A month later a friend came to see him. The professor had invited the friend to dinner. The professor struck the boy "as an odd one," and knowing that Vicki's father had eaten at the professor's house, he asked if he should accept the invitation. "By all means," Vicki's father said emphatically; "the man is a magnificent cook, and the evening will be a night to remember. Dessert in particular will be an astonishing surprise."

Late in February I forsook the terrace and the *Horchow Garden* for the season itself. During a February thaw the earth absorbed snow, and hills melted out of brittleness. In the woods lumps of snow lingered, resembling quartz boulders shouldering upward out of the ground. Juncos blew about like dust, and winds rattled red pines, shaking cones off branches. Beside a road a stand of paperbark birch saplings was suddenly noticeable. Trunks of the trees leaned out from the dark woods in slow curves. Once the trunks slid free from the shadow of the forest, they swept skyward. From a distance the saplings resembled streams of milk trickling down the sides of a gray jug. Some afternoons snow swirled like italics. In the abandoned wolf pen British soldiers bloomed atop a tattered log shelter, tips of the lichens glowing like scarlet helmets.

When examining the Horchow catalog, I imagined sitting on the terrace and reading the mail. I soon decided, however, that my correspondence was too informal for a courtyard. From Las Vegas, a "sophomore at Chaparral High School" wrote, saying she had a "very serious passion for the Disney character Goofy." "I would deeply appreciate it," she said, "if you could send me some information on your line of work that would enhance my research." The only goofy thing in my life, I told the girl, was "an imaginary terrace, not something that would enhance your research." Strangers often send me stories, urging me to use them in essays. The stories I received in February were too rude not only for my books but also for the *Horchow Garden* with its pages prim with faux topiaries and porcelain dessert plates. From Kentucky a woman mailed me a folk tale, "a comboberation," she explained, "of bull cat and snake bite." The woman had recently gone through a divorce, probably a rancorous one. The tale was familiar. I had heard it four times in Tennessee and once in both Virginia and Arkansas. All the people who told it to me were women, and the story seems to be a woman's tale. In Connecticut I tried it on two female acquaintances, one a kindergarten teacher, the other a senior vice president of an insurance company. Before I reached the second paragraph, both women interrupted me, saying they had heard the story many times.

A woman in Campbellsburg, my correspondent recounted, lived with a worthless husband. He drank, chewed tobacco, and bayed after every female Southern Cur in northwest Kentucky.

Exasperated by the man's shiftlessness, the woman decided to leave him. Her husband's birthday was approaching, however, and before decamping the woman wanted to buy him a present he would never forget and that would pay him back for subjecting her to years of indignities. Accordingly she visited the zoo in Cincinnati. Occasionally the zoo sold surplus animals to pet collectors, and the woman hoped that amid the stinking and stinging creations, she could find a memorable pet for her husband. The zoo director offered her an electric eel, a pair of mole rats, and a marabou stork that stank like a septic tank. Nothing, though, was bad enough for the woman's husband. For a while the woman thought about purchasing a hyena puppy and telling her husband that it was a new strain of Treeing Tennessee Brindle. "Haven't you got anything worse?" the woman asked as she watched the puppy gnaw the head off one of its litter mates. "Just one thing," the director said. "We have tried to give it away for years, but no one will take it." "Show me the creature," the woman said. The director led her down two flights of stairs to a tunnel resembling a bomb shelter. At the end of the tunnel stood a massive steel door with seven bolts stitched across the front. After the director unlocked the door, he led the woman into a cavernous room. Pushed into one corner of the room was an ancient safe, too heavy to move, the director explained. In the middle of the room stood a wooden chair. In the seat of the chair was a creature the size of a cantaloupe sliced in two, hair rumpling over it, making it look like a kitchen mop. Aside from the hair no other part of the creature was visible, "no head, no eyes, no feet, no tail, no nothing," my correspondent wrote. "What in the name of goodness is that?" the woman whispered. "It's a furburger," the director said. "What does it do?" the woman asked. "Watch this," the director replied, turning toward the chair. "Furburger," he shouted, "the safe!" Immediately the creature sprang from the chair and flew at the safe roaring like the Seven Vampire Winds. Dust billowed, and the woman coughed and shut her eyes for a moment. When she opened them again, the furburger was back in the chair, and the safe had vanished. In its place was a mound of shards, not one of them bigger than a toy soldier. "I'll take it," the woman said. That night when her husband staggered home from an evening spent swilling corn juice at Bubba's New Ring Café, the furburger was in the middle of the kitchen table. "What the hell is that?" the husband said, leaning over a chair and staring bleary-eyed at the centerpiece. "Darling," the woman said sweetly, "that's a furburger." "A what?" the man exclaimed, rubbing his nose. "Dearest, that's a furburger," the woman answered; "it's your birthday present." "Furburger, my ass!" the man exclaimed.

"That story," Josh said, "won't mix with limestone and laven-der." In the same mail I received a letter from Coker Knox in Nashville. Coker had just completed another course in poetry writing at the YMCA night school. "Come to Tennessee," he wrote, "and you and I will sit upon the soft *anthoxanthum odoratum* that covers the blushing sod and listen to the harmonious utterances of the fluttering world made vocal." The verdigris that colored the bench on my terrace was not so green or fragrant as Coker's sweet vernal grass. Suddenly I longed for Carthage and the country characters who bumble through my essays. Carthage lay just beyond the gate on my terrace wall. Perhaps real benches exist only in the mind, not in catalogs or on terraces. In any case, I was soon lounging on a bench outside the Smith County Courthouse, listening to a menagerie of animal stories.

Last fall when Brother John Sankey's "Animals of Zion" exhibition came to Carthage, boys at the school for the afflicted in Buffalo Valley were given a holiday. Although the exhibition contained an assortment of gospel creatures, including, among others, a baby elephant, a lion that had lost its tail, four penguins, and a crate of copperheads and rattlesnakes, the highlight of the show was a family of baboons. In the spring hogs broke into Juno Feathers's chicken coop and ate all the chickens. Brother John said he would repair the wire around the coop if Juno would let him house his baboons in her barnyard. Juno agreed, and for the five days the exhibition stayed in Carthage, the barnyard attracted every layabout in Smith County. Loafers leaned against the wire and threw apple cores and orange peels at the baboons. They taunted the animals, witticisms such as "you're one" and "you're one, too" never failing to elicit guffaws of laughter. One afternoon an inmate from the school approached the barnyard as the loafers were roaring with laughter, one of their number having shouted "so's your mother" at a baboon. "Is it nice to laugh at strangers who don't understand English?" the man from the school said. "If you were in their country, would you like them to laugh at you? You are behaving like apes, not Christians, and I think you owe these visitors an apology. It's bad enough that the Walton Hotel is filled because of the exhibition and these folks have to stay in a chicken house."

That same day Hoben Donkin ate lunch at Ankerrow's Café. Several inmates from the school also ate in the café. "Yesterday in the woods near Maggart," Hoben said, "I saw two black bears fighting." "Which bear won?" one of the inmates asked. "I don't know," Hoben said. "How could you see a fight and not know who won?" the inmate continued. "When I watch a fight, I always know the winner." "I saw who won," Hoben said, a touch of gravel in his voice, "but how can I tell you? One of the bears wasn't wearing red overalls, and the other, boots and an orange shirt." "That's neither here nor over yonder," the man said. "Everybody knows bears don't wear clothes. What do shirts and overalls have to do with it anyhow? I just asked you which of the bears won the fight. If you can't answer a civil question, then you can go to hell."

Before Hoben could respond, Piety Goforth's brother Orfeeus stumbled into the café. Nobody in Smith County played the fiddle better than Orfeeus, especially old lowdown tunes like "Pecker on a Pole" and "Mamma Don't 'Low No Diddlin' Here." Orfeeus was quarrelsome, however, and his wife, Eunice, left him. "It's no wonder Eunice moved out," Turlow Gutheridge said, "Orfeeus is so mean he'd wrestle a water moccasin and give the snake the first bite." Despite his musical talent, Orfeeus was not sensitive. Turlow said he was descended from the dwarves who once peopled Tennessee. Cherokee Indians chased the dwarves away. Because the dwarves were half-wood and half-flesh, the Indians struggled. Every time a Cherokee shot an arrow or swung a club at a dwarf, the dwarf turned his wooden side toward the arrow. Only when Indians started using hatchets and began chopping the dwarves into kindling, did dwarves leave Tennessee.

Be that as it may, however, when Orfeeus entered the café, he shook like he was suffering from distemper. He had spent the previous week at Dapper Tuttlebee's still. On the way back to Carthage, Orfeeus recounted, he passed a strange house. Dogs were everywhere. "Bull dogs, cow dogs, fox and possum terriers, a sausage dog bigger than a ham, black and white dogs, pink and green dogs. A pack of drunken beagles in a peach tree, rabbits sitting on their heads. A coonhound hunched on the ridge pole of the house. A bloodhound squatted on the privy, the door wide open. A boxer cranked buckets up and down in the well, a Boston terrier in one bucket, a Memphis terrier in the other." "All the dogs were howling," Orfeeus said, "and I tried to slink past the house, but one of these here Swiss dogs with a whiskey barrel around its neck saw me and trotted out to the road. 'Stop,' he barked, standing on his hind legs and putting his right paw on my shoulder. 'When you get to the next house, go inside and tell the dog who lives there that Billy Braxton died.'" "The next house," Orfeeus continued, "was a tarpaper shack, but I did what the foreigner asked me to do. I went inside. The chinches bit something terrible, and the fireplace smoked so bad I couldn't see at first. So many bones were on the floor that I thought I had stumbled into a slaughter house. Finally, I spotted a mangy yellow dog lying on a pile of straw. His ribs stuck out like fish hooks, and his eyes were as blurry as peanut butter soup. 'Heyo, good buddy,' I said, 'the fellow up the road told me to tell you that Billy Braxton was dead.' 'Hot damn,' the dog yipped, jumping up and running out the door. 'By God, I'll be king yet.'"

My taste in stories is not genteel. Although the new terrace was attractive, I preferred sitting on the bench outside the courthouse. In the fall the Tennessee legislature debated legalizing horse-racing, and Slubey Garts preached a lovefest of sermons damning gambling. "Not to mix barns," Turlow Gutheridge said, "but nobody knows how to milk the sacred cow better than Slubey." "Few people," Slubey himself said, "are reliable enough to ride herd on themselves." The races were to be held in Nashville. After the last bets were paid, Slubey predicted, Carthaginians would find themselves "in the Dreamland Hotel cantering poisonous pastures with Yolanda and Juanita." Slubey did not criticize the mule races held at the Smith County fair. "A mule will carry you," he said, "but a horse will throw you." Legalized gambling, he declared, would bring Satan's Triple Crown to Tennessee, "The Moloch Derby, the Belial Stakes, and the Mammon." "In the race of life, the post horn is tuned to the sound of salvation and the Christian wears God's sacramental colors. The Weeping Cross not the half-mile pole points the way to heaven." "God," Slubey said, "will harness the sinner with doctrine, slap a preacher on his conscience, put blinders on his pride and pull him into church, but then the sinner has got to feel fire behind him and gallop for Glory."

My mind shifts back and forth between fiction and nonfiction. In March I imagined Slubey coming to Storrs and, if not sitting on the terrace and admiring the frangipani, at least eating dinner with Vicki and the children and me. Seated beside the children at the table, Slubey would not have mentioned the fleshpots of Nashville. Instead, aphorisms would have punctuated his conversation, periods and exclamation marks being replaced with statements such as "the fish goes after the bait, not the hook" or "he who mocks the crooked man had better walk straight."

Slubey did not visit. An opportunity to buy a radio station arose, and he stayed in Carthage to complete the purchase. Slubey now owns WGOD. Every Sunday night he produces a show, *The Evening Star Gospel and Holiness Hour.* For my part I am glad Slubey did not visit. In fact I spent little time on the terrace in March. I like the whimsical March snows. One day snow falls in patties; the next afternoon flurries scud across fields, the flakes splinters twirling yellow and blue in the sunlight. Many people dislike the ash end of winter, and as snow piled up, people in Connecticut drifted into irritation. Deceptive breezes from the south had softened them. Scarlet threads atop beaked hazelnut and red-winged blackbirds made people dream of hibiscus and palm, slack blue nights and days sagging comfortably like hammocks. In November cold was a tonic, invigorating and firming steps. In March ice floes in the blood no longer quickened, and instead of appreciating the immediate, conversations celebrated the faraway, Florida and the Caribbean, spongy, vague places, oozing lethargy and warmth.

I walked through early March. One morning after seven inches of snow, I took George and Penny to the woods. Penny bounced through the snow, pronging like a small antelope. Long and low, George battered his way. After two hours, his back legs folded, and he collapsed in a heap. I carried him home. "George is old," Vicki said, taking him in her arms, "and you've killed him." "He is my dog," I said. "If I want to kill him, I can." After Vicki and the children piled hot water bottles around him, George recovered.

In March ice storms turned field and wood to tinsel. Strips of ice bound the skeletons of last summer's plants. Beside paths saplings snapped in the wind while in the woods trees clacked together, peeling ice from one another, the ice falling in curls then skittering across the frozen ground. On European weeping birch limbs swayed and tinkled like silver bells. Old leaves dangling from beeches twisted into caramel cones, ice covering them in thin translucent layers resembling melted sugar. Under the ice buds on cornelian cherries beamed red and orange. On spice-bush flower buds looked like green knapsacks. Beneath ice cat-kins on willows resembled thready silk pearls. Ice starched black birch into formality, the herringbone pattern on catkins suddenly visible. Often I walked at night. Lights from the university shined through trees, turning top branches into silver veils. Behind the limbs the sky was blue-brown, clouds separating out in loose creamy bundles.

On icy days I did not sit on the terrace. In fact I probably won't spend much time on the terrace until next February. Yesterday was the first day of spring. Daffodils are pushing up in the dell. Fourteen robins dropped into the backyard this morning. An hour ago I got my pond net down from the rafters in the garage. March snows have melted, and I hope spotted salamanders will soon appear in the beaver pond. Only once have I seen a spotted sala-mander, and I would trade a good portion of the furniture on the terrace for a glimpse of another salamander, say, maybe the bench and two of the chairs.

THE EDGE OF SPRING

Near the end of March I flew to Florida to address a seminar of commercial real estate brokers. The brokers gathered at the Grenelefe Golf and Tennis Resort near Haines City. The seminar lasted three and a half days. The brokers began work at seven in the morning and ended early in the afternoon, so people could fish or play golf. Since I only spoke once to the seminar, I had much free time. "You'll get a jump on spring," Vicki said, as she packed my suitcase. "Bring a greenhouse back to Connecticut." I followed Vicki's instructions. Mornings and afternoons I wandered the resort, looking at plants and animals.

Fruit ripened on loquats, ballooning orange and lumpy from the ends of twigs. Bees washed through elderberry, sweeping up nectar and shaking across flower clusters like small unstable puddles. On hawthorn flowers bloomed in minute settings of cups and saucers. From black cherries blossoms dangled in tired brushes. Having just hatched, tent caterpillars wrinkled into the cherries, resembling seams thick with bristles. On live oaks the edges of leaves crinkled, almost as if they had been wrapped around curling irons. Oak leaves rotted slowly, and in the scrub they covered the ground like granola. From the oaks knots of moss draped bleached, looking like water-logged fish nets.

On "Canaan Farm Lands," just off Lake Marion Road, red cattle munched palmetto leaves. Egrets followed the cattle, stabbing at insects stirred by the animals' hooves. Breeding had started, and plumes of orange feathers swept brushed over the heads and down the necks of the egrets. One afternoon I left Grenelefe and walked along Lake Marion Road. Three golf courses wound through the resort, and fairways and roadsides were manicured. Along shoulders of roads in the resort stood signs, white squares of cardboard with green letters stamped on them. "Pesticide Application," the signs warned. "Keep Off Until Dry." In the center of each sign was a circle with a line resembling a closed gate drawn across it. Behind the gate stood a stick man. On the man's left lurked a child. In his right hand the man held a leash that stretched down to the outline of a Scottie dog.

Just seeing a warning about poison made my nose run, and so I walked along Lake Marion Road in hopes of escaping the pesticide. Fields were splotched. Hooves of the cattle dug up grass, and sand bulged and spilled out. In shadows the sand was blue and resembled granite boulders rolling under a Connecticut hillside. From a corner of a field a buzzard lumbered into flight, and I watched him beat upward into a thermal. Unfortunately, I did not gaze skyward long. Florida does not have a bottle-return law, and the shoulder of the road looked like an aging landfill. Beer cans jutted through the sand like edges of an underground metallic ledge. While plastic bags snagged then tattered on the barbed wire fence surrounding Canaan Lands, a bale of paper crumpled out of print and sank into the ground. I picked up a scrap. Measuring four-and-a-half-by-two-inches, the scrap was a ticket for the Florida lottery. The ticket cost a dollar and was for a game entitled "FIRST-N-TEN." A person could, the ticket proclaimed, "WIN UP TO $500!" Sketched on the left front of the ticket were five football players. The players had huge forearms and skinny calves. All wore white pants, blue jerseys with white stripes running along the shoulders, and pointy blue and white helmets. Most of the print had rubbed off the ticket. Still visible on the back, though, was the name of the secretary of the Florida lottery. The secretary was a woman. Printed after her name was "Ph.D." "Good Lord," I mumbled. "I prefer pesticide to this poison."

I stuffed the ticket into my pocket and returned to Grenelefe. Cabbage palms towered over palmettos. The fan-shaped leaves of the palms bent outward, segments rising then suddenly tipping over like feathers broken near trailing edges. Muscadine grape wound through thickets, the vines drooping into swings. Cords of Virginia creeper wrapped around trunks of longleaf pine. The pines grew throughout the resort. The trees were elegant, and often I sat on the ground and stared at them. Candles burned silver and yellow amid tufts of needles. Over a foot long, needles burst up in green fountains then splashed down shimmering in the light. The pines stood out against the sky, white clouds blowing above them like plumes of smoke, the sky itself a huge porcelain snuffer curving over the candles.

Ribbons of Japanese photina wrapped around buildings, new leaves spiraling in red blades. Philodendron grew in the middle of divided roads. Leaf scars on the plants formed ovals resembling eyes. From the top of each scar glared a black pupil, while sharp hairs surrounded the scars like eyelashes. In the brush chameleons established territories. Usually they clung to saplings, tails higher than heads, the heads themselves jutting out like remnants of branches snapped by wind. When disturbed, a chameleon skittered then bounded like a frog. Rarely did a chameleon shift from one tree to another. Beneath the jaw of each chameleon was a grainy orange pouch. When hanging upside down, chameleons inflated then quickly deflated the pouches, the orange flicking and vanishing like drops of rain dripping from the ends of twigs. Above the chameleons solitary carpenter bees established territories. Hovering ten feet over the ground, the bees appeared lumbering and awkward, at least until intruders violated their territories. Then the bees dropped like blades and swung after intruders, chasing them away. Aside from gray squirrels, a feral dog lurking at the edge of a parking lot, and armadillos who shuffled along fairways early in the morning, I saw no four-legged animals.

In mornings Carolina wrens called from thickets. The birds perched near the ends of stubby, broken limbs and were not noticeable until they sang, their breasts suddenly swelling orange. At night whippoorwills called, their songs mingling in the dark with the soft potpourri of orange blossoms. Early one morning a red-shouldered hawk clung like a shadow to the top of a dead pine. Outside the conference center Brewer's blackbirds ranged through grass, rummaging for scraps. Brown thrashers and rufous-sided towhees scratched through underbrush, and red-bellied woodpeckers swooped across lawns "churring," the sound resembling a starter cord being pulled on a lawn mower.

Many birds were common residents of Connecticut: titmice, cardinals, blue jays, and crows, although the cries of this last quavered more than the calls of crows in Storrs, making them sound like ducks. Mockingbirds jabbered through afternoons while catbirds mewed amid tangles of grape and cherry. Mockingbirds had already appeared in Storrs, but catbirds would not appear until forsythia bloomed. Yellow-rumped warblers flitted through live oaks. In May they would be common in Storrs, bouncing above Schoolhouse Brook, the yellow in their tails almost clicking in the sunlight. Early in the morning a flock of sandhill cranes flew to the driving range at the resort, their spindly legs wobbling behind them. Never had I seen sandhill cranes, and I watched them for a long time, marveling at the slow elegance of their walk and the feathers folded over their sides in silky layers. Courtship displays were common. The cranes flapped their wings, lowered their heads, and pranced up and down, making me imagine them square dancers strutting higher than fiddles.

Spring did not accompany me back to Storrs. I arrived home on a gray day. The only plant in bloom was the silver torch cactus in the study of my friend Josh. Red tubes erupted from the sides of columns like scarlet water bursting out of rotten pipes. Florida, however, had brought spring to mind, so in hopes of forcing the season I spent a day in Hampton, Connecticut, at Trail Wood, the home of Edwin Way Teale, the naturalist. I roamed Trail Wood, but no matter where I looked, spring seemed distant. A stand of quaking aspen beside Hampton Brook was blue and frozen. A pair of mallards drifted sleepily across the beaver pond, and the "Hyla Pond" was silent. Shells of skunk cabbage crept across wetlands, the spikes not yet rank with blossoms. On the right of way of the abandoned railroad owl pellets sagged into cinders.

Although spring had not blown up from the south and drizzled across Trail Wood, hints of change were apparent at home. Edward tried out for two baseball teams and began tennis lessons. For her part Eliza signed up for both soccer and softball. Educators began to dream of greener intellectual times, and in hopes of invigorating depleted resources, colleges searched for fertile presidents. As usual I was nominated for a presidency or two, a matter to which I paid little attention. Of more importance was a hatching of carpenter ants. One day ants streamed from under the baseboard in Vicki's and my bedroom. I bought two gallons of insecticide, Ortho's Home Defense, and that afternoon sprayed the foundations of the house.

After April arrived, I spent more time drinking coffee and eavesdropping on conversations at the Cup of Sun. One morning I heard a woman say to a companion, "the evil spirits, the demons, take the appearance of. . . ." I did not hear the last word of the sentence. On the edge of spring, however, the incomplete often appeals more than the complete. As spicebush unraveled into yellow flowers, I imaged story, ordinary details suddenly blossoming into colorful fiction. Unfinished stories bloomed at the edge of spring. Josh also went to Florida in March. On the flight home, a mild woman sat next to him on the airplane. "All that sunlight," Josh said, made him blossom, more like a skunk cabbage, however, than any other flower. Before the flight left Orlando the stewardess explained the use of seat belts and oxygen masks. "I was rested," Josh said, "and I listened to the explanations." When the stewardess described the bathrooms on the plane, she said, "all lavatories are equipped with smoke detectors." "Smoke detectors! What about toilets!" Josh exclaimed, addressing the woman sitting beside him. "I don't give a shit about smoke detectors. I think privies ought to have toilets." Although startled by the rough take-off, the woman quickly recovered. To fly to Hartford, Josh changed planes in Raleigh, North Carolina. The woman got off the plane in Raleigh. She lived just across the North Carolina line in Virginia, and as she and Josh trudged into the terminal, she turned to him and said, "Flying from hot Florida to cold Connecticut could undermine someone's health. Virginia is a temperate, in-between place. Why don't you spend a few days with me and warm up before you go to Connecticut?" Josh, unfortunately, relishes shocks, cold showers, and steamy words, and he continued on to Hartford, leaving me to imagine what might have happened.

Many of the brokers in Florida were southern, and at dinner under the sunny influence of wine, stories bloomed. The stories were silly tales without bite or sting, stories that made fun of the narrator rather than other people. In a discussion of songs a man from Birmingham mentioned *Yankee Doodle Dandy*. In Alabama, he said, "most people sing the old version that begins, 'Yank my doodle. It's a dandy.'" "Outside Naples a new golf course was just finished," a man from Florida recounted. Problems bedeviled the construction, one of which was a small graveyard on the site planned for the fourteenth green. The builder bought land for a new graveyard after which he won approval for moving the coffins by agreeing to erect an obelisk over each grave. Still, moving the bodies disturbed people, particularly old Mrs. Shugrue. Her husband Artemus died nine years ago, and she planned to be buried next to him. "I've got some funeral rights," she said. "I don't want no mistakes. I couldn't bear to be laid out next to one of those Teesels. They are as common as pig tracks." To make sure that corpses were not mixed up, Mrs. Shugrue asked her son-in-law to supervise Artemus's journey. Not only that but to insure that the corpse was Artemus, she instructed her son-in-law to open the coffin before it was buried in the new plot. "The turkey buzzard," she said, speaking of the builder, "doesn't guard the corpse."

Mrs. Shugrue's son-in-law followed her instructions, and on the afternoon he returned from the graveyard, Mrs. Shugrue was waiting for him on the front porch. "Did you watch them dig up the box?" she asked. "Yes," he said, striding up the steps and hurrying into the kitchen to wash his hands, before going into the tool shed and removing a jar of whiskey from behind a can of nails. "Did you make sure they stuck the box in the right hole?" Mrs. Shugrue asked. "Yes," the son-in-law answered, rolling his eyes and pouring a glass two-thirds full of whiskey down his throat. "Did you ask them to open the coffin?" Mrs. Shugrue said. "Yes," her son-in-law answered, looking distractedly into the distance. "Did you see Pappy?" Mrs. Shugrue then said. "Yes," the man answered. "Well, then, how did the dear soul look?" Mrs. Shugrue said beaming with pleasure. "Poorly," the son-in-law said, leaning against the porch railing and spitting hard against a palmetto.

In spring time escalates, making people so aware of mortality that they pause and reminisce. In telling anecdotes about family people bridle the irregular thump of change. One man at the seminar spent his childhood in Morristown, Tennessee. His family was poor, and to earn spending money he collected scrap iron. A wagonload of iron was worth seventy-five cents, "big money," he said, "when a movie ticket cost ten cents." One day near the train station he found a blue plate that had slipped out of a crate being loaded onto a boxcar. "I had never seen anything so lovely," the man said. "The plate was bluer than the sky. I took it home, and Mother put it on the mantle over the fireplace. On holidays Mother let me eat off the plate. Because I found the plate, my cousins said I was special. Actually, the plate made me think I was special. When I gazed at the plate, blue swept over me."

The story itself resembled a plate, one that I filled with side dishes, accounts of doings that I wanted to describe but did not think nourishing enough for an essay. While winter demands hearty stories that stick to ribs, the edge of spring is narrow, best-suited to tidbits. Some years ago the neighbor of one of my Tennessee friends started building a swimming pool in his backyard. "My pool will make yours look like a sink," the neighbor told my friend. The goose ought not to tweak the nose of the sleeping fox. One afternoon my friend drove to the stockyards and filled the trunk of his car with cow bones. That night he crept into his neighbor's yard and tossed the bones into the hole being dug for the pool. He also hired the services of two "defrocked" Indians. The next morning when the neighbor awoke, he looked out his window. The Indians were marching back and forth along the road in front of his house. Each carried a sign reading, "Desecration of Native American Burial Ground. Stop the Construction *Now*."

Pranks usually violate good taste. As a result they are side dishes, pastries that slip quickly out of mind and are recalled only rarely, when, for example, a blue dish makes a person hanker for a forgotten home. A while ago some Nashvillians hunted deer in North Carolina. Just as a man aimed his gun at a big buck, a yellow mongrel broke cover and bounded toward the deer. The buck bolted. Angry, the hunter shifted his gun and shot the dog. Quietly a friend of mine paid the guide to come back later and collect the dog's body. Afterward my friend had the dog stuffed. One Saturday when the hunter left town for a weekend, my friend, accompanied by a carpenter, slipped into the man's house and bolted the stuffed dog to the wall above the fireplace in the living room.

In preparing books for the market, essayists often remove the giblets. At the end of March I stirred the past, searching for gizzard and heart, tales that would season gray days. Ten or so years ago a friend started a business in Nashville. To make the business successful the man practically lived in his office, in the process neglecting his children and "not," his wife, Clara, said, "paying me the attention due a southern lady." From a neighbor Clara borrowed a big silver platter. She set the platter in the middle of the dining-room table. On the platter she heaped lettuce: leaf, Bibb, romaine, and iceberg. Around the lip of the platter she piled vegetables: tomatoes, green onions, peas, asparagus, spinach, and celery. Atop the vegetables she sliced hard-boiled eggs. Beside the platter she set a dish of corn cakes. Lastly, in the middle of the platter she arranged the main course. When her husband walked through the front door, Clara greeted him, sitting on the platter, looking like a Thanksgiving turkey, all feathers and clothing removed, pink paper ruffles on her wrists and ankles.

"I love to tell the story," the old hymn declares, "Of unseen things above, / Of Jesus and His glory, / Of Jesus and His love." For my part I love to tell stories of love below. For readers longing for a mild spring, my tales are a little strong. I am afraid, however, that I like powerful fragrances. Not for me zephyrs dripping camphor and myrrh but a kitchen heavy with the perfume of boiled cabbage and hambone. Occasionally I ponder telling higher stories. Rarely do I ponder long. My way to glory wanders the low narrative ground. Shortly after leaving Florida, I thought about Slubey Garts, owner of and preacher at the Tabernacle of Love. Sometimes Slubey slipped on integrity. Rarely did he distribute loaves and fishes widely. But he was not so acquisitive as rival divines alleged, saying that "anyone who shakes hands with Slubey had better count his fingers afterward."

In February Slubey bought a radio station, WGOD. On Sunday nights the station broadcast Slubey's *Evening Star Gospel and Holiness Hour.* The program was a miscellany, consisting of obituaries; announcements of deaths and births; a list of hospital admissions and discharges; a segment entitled "Songs of Salvation," consisting of old hymns; a sermon by Slubey; and then "He Will Pilot Thee," the testimonial of a reformed sinner. The program was wildly popular in Smith County, the testimonials generally being scandalous and the hymns rousing favorites, standbys like "Softly and Tenderly," "Heaven's Fair City," "Blessed Assurance," "Now the Day Is Over," and "Tell Mother I'll Be There."

"Fleshing out the bones of platitude with the Spirit," as Turlow Gutheridge put it, Slubey's sermons were short exhortations, quickened around such maxims as "curiosity fills the mousetrap" and "now is yesterday's tomorrow." Proverbs Goforth, deacon of the Tabernacle of Love, assisted Slubey during the broadcast, reading obituaries and hospital admissions then announcing local events, such things as the grand opening of Sister Ramona Jaxson's beauty parlor, La Belle de Beaucoup de Fashionette on Spring Street. The deacon's English was more inspirational than grammatical, and his descriptions of medical doings enlivened Gray's dull *Anatomy*. Bilbo Hubbs, the deacon reported, was "infested with a conglomeration of rectangular and postulated infirmities, his left lung being abnormally epitomized." On births and deaths the deacon did slightly better. When Capri Scates got drunk then burned himself up while smoking in bed, the deacon reported that Capri "died suddenly in a mattress fire." Emma Ruth Bramlett, the deacon recounted, "gave birth to twins last Thursday morning after a long and difficult labor. According to Doctor Sollows, the tiny juveniles were as hard to extract as ingrowing teeth." "Anyway, one of them is a boy and the other is a girl," the deacon said, pausing for a moment before continuing, a tremor of doubt in his voice, "or maybe it's the other way around."

The highlight of each broadcast was the testimonial of a repentant sinner. Sometimes people recounted reaping what they sowed, or, as the deacon phrased it, "bringing obstruction down upon their own heads." Other times they described the shady practices of "Pilate's Hall," forsaken as soon as they "basked in the sunshine of the King's love." Last week's repentant follower of the Lamb was Brother John Sankey. Brother John traveled Tennessee, Kentucky, and Missouri, exhibiting his "Animals of Zion." He brought his show to Carthage for five days, and on the broadcast he described the deceptions of an earlier, unsanctified career. At that time his most popular exhibit was the body of a mermaid. Bedouins found the body of the mermaid on the eastern shore of the Dead Sea, John told people, "not far from the place where the corpse of Jozrah, the old Hebrew, washed ashore."

"Anyone who tells the truth ought to keep one foot in the stirrup," John said. "Lies strapped the feedbag to my horse and kept me rocking on the porch." Jozrah taught dancing "to the gals in Pharaoh's harem, the schottish or camel trot, whatever they done back yonder." When the call came summoning the Israelites to Canaan, Jozrah malingered in Goshen, delaying his departure in order to enjoy a last quickstep with Floy, his favorite dancer. By the time Jozrah started across the Red Sea, the other Israelites had disappeared into the Wilderness. Before Jozrah reached Sinai, the flood, John declared, "poured over him like a trumpet blowing 'Be Left. Away. Terrible Day. It's Too Late To Pray.'"

In reality the body of the mermaid was that of Sunflower, a baboon that died from trichinosis. Brother John's first cousin worked for Frosty Morn hams. After Sunflower's death, the cousin cured her body in the company's smokehouse in Lebanon. A week later John took his show to Cowan, Tennessee. Blue laws prevented him from displaying his creatures on Sunday, and he spent the day touring the college at Sewanee. Among objects in a display case in the science building, John told listeners to WGOD, was "a jar containing a baby floating in naugahyde." After the tour John returned to the science building and stole the baby. "I sawed off the head," he said, "and then throwed the rest of the baby down a well." John's cousin at Frosty Morn peeled the head of a duroc hog and sent John the skin. "I needed the face of a duroc," John explained, "because the skin of a duroc is red, and Bible mermaids all have suntans." As soon as he received the skin, John pulled it down over the skull of the baby attaching it to the jawbones with safety pins.

The next Sunday John went fishing, explaining that it wasn't a sin to fish on the Sabbath because that was when God talked to him. John caught a string of carp. Before cooking the fish, he cut off their fins. After dinner he took all the makings—head, fins, and smoked baboon—to his grandmother. For several years running her antimacassars had won blue ribbons at the Tennessee State Fair. Two days later the mermaid was finished. Braids of fins ran down Sunflower's arms and legs, and the baby's skull sat atop the baboon's body. John's grandmother kept Sunflower's real head, storing it in a cookie jar in the pantry, explaining that "such a thing might come in handy some day."

The needlework was so carefully done that the stitches never needed tightening. Curing Sunflower, however, turned her backside red. "Aside," John said, "from covering her behind with black shoe polish when it got scuffed and shaking a few moth balls into her bed during summer months, the mermaid was maintenance-free." Although John still carried Sunflower with him on his travels, he had not exhibited her in years. For Slubey, however, John agreed to let Sunflower's light shine at the "Sweet Hour of Prayer" meeting on Wednesday night at the Tabernacle of Love. The mermaid's appearance caused a sensation, quadrupling attendance at the meeting. The evening was so successful that Slubey held an "Enfolded in the Everlasting Arms" encore the next night. At both services Sunflower lay in a child's coffin by the Mourner's bench, a yellow bow pinned to her snout. Tied to the brass fixings on the coffin were helium balloons, most pink, but three pink and spotted with purple, and one, if Turlow Gutheridge is to be believed, advertising the Hermitage Hotel in Nashville. Pasted on the wall behind the bench were pictures drawn by first-graders in the Carthage School. The best picture depicted Sunflower in heaven, her snout a long Roman nose, her fins angelic golden wings, and her hair piled brown at her feet, her body having been shampooed in the Blood of the Lamb. Before the offering the congregation filed past the deceased. Tears flowed like the River Jordan. Cloudina Teague wept so hard she fainted and had to be dragged out of the Tabernacle.

In Storrs not rain but snow fell from the clouds. Early in April days seemed to slide off the edge of spring into the season itself. Ice disappeared from brooks, and stained by tannic acid, roots of yellow birch bloomed orange underwater. Wood frogs laid gelatinous clumps of eggs in spring pools. Deer ticks reappeared, and buds of rose azalea swelled white and red, ready to explode. The Saturday before Easter Vicki, the children, and I dyed eggs. Well, to be accurate, the children and I colored eggs while Vicki supervised and kept us clean. Before she dyed her eggs, Eliza drew pictures on the shells with crayons: flags twisting in breezes, flowers, leafy vines, and on one egg a green Cyclops with a nose shaped like an eggplant. Vicki said the decorations mirrored our personalities. Bands of pastel neat as hedgerows circled Edward's eggs while color plashed down from the large to the small ends of Francis's eggs in shaky ripples. In contrast color splotched my eggs, evoking, Vicki said, the Mediterranean, the south of France, and the "blobby nature of your essays."

Easter morning was rainy, so the Easter Bunny turned the house into an egg warren. In the afternoon rain changed to snow. The next morning two inches of damp snow blanketed trees. The trees looked as if they were wearing long white gloves, the limbs forearms and the twigs fingers. "The woods drank milk," a student said. "The white on branches," she explained, resembled mustaches, "the spray that clings to a child's upper lip after she gulps down a glass of milk." Time was pulling the curtain that separated winter from spring. To me the snow seemed dust stirred during spring cleaning. In order not to miss the end of winter, I got up early and roamed the woods. "I don't know how many more times I will see such beauty," I told Vicki, adding that "dead folks usually don't wander far from their graves, even after snowstorms."

Three days later eighteen inches of snow fell. The university canceled classes, and I spent the morning meandering wood and field. The snow jerked at my boots like undertow, and gusts broke across my face like waves slapping a beach. Walking resembled swimming, and I swung my arms and kicked through drifts. At times I imagined myself under water. Snow piled atop the limbs of sugar maples, turning trees into white ledges of staghorn coral. The limbs of weeping Higan cherry spread in delicate fans. The storm transformed the tulip tree in front of Gulley Hall into a white log that seemed to float through distance. Snow encased branches, whitewashing them and making them appear crinkles on a sandy beach. On the northeast side of the tree, a thick current of snow streamed down the middle of the trunk. At the sides of the trunk, the snow warped away, exposing bark and planing the tree into definition. Buds on saucer magnolia bent upward, resembling clutches of bleached mudsnails, snow catching between them sandy and heavy. Snow did not stick to the seed pods of Kentucky coffee trees, and the pods swirled skyward like schools of dark anemone fish. Catkins on willows around Unnamed Pond gleamed yellow through the snow, reminding me of butterfly fish turning in the sun. Bunches of cones on alders shook in the wind and resembled roe caught in the froth of waves.

I trudged up the hill through the Storrs Community Cemetery. Tops of stones jutted through drifts like shattered hunks of coral. At least the stones were dead until I read names engraved upon them. Names quickened the graveyard: Fuller, Dunham, Barrows, Henderson, Freeman, Whitney, and then appropriate to the day, Snow and Starkweather. A red obelisk towered above Edwin Whitney, who founded "The Connecticut Soldiers' Orphan Home By A Gift Of All His Property For The Benefit Of Soldiers And Their Orphans." Emily Starkweather's husband, John Day, fought in the Civil War, serving in "Company A 1st Conn. Heavy Artillery." I looked up from the stone. Across the graveyard a robin flew into a sumac and pecked at an old fruit. A clump of snow tumbled from a cornelian cherry. Cherries were blooming, and the flowers resembled hunks of butter floating through a churn.

By noon melting began. After two days the snow was gone. After class I walked behind the sheep barns. Peepers called from a pool. At the edge of woods along the cut for the power line, a man pushed leaves aside, searching for ivy. He wore short pants, a light sweater, and Wellington boots. "The season is changing," he said, standing up, "spring is winging up from the south." A mockingbird racketed from a fence post. "Yes," I said, the sky curving above me like a blue plate.

SPRING RUNNING

               The rain fell in panes. When the panes hit the ground, they shattered into slivers, spearing dirt then pushing it into the woods behind the house. Clumps of leaves washed across Hillside Circle and tumbled into the ditch that sliced through the dell. Roots snared leaves; dikes formed, and water rolled over my daffodils in silver circles. Four times during the afternoon I shoveled leaves from the ditch. "The blow has just started," Josh said over the telephone. "The center of the storm is over Mt. Ararat. You better send Vicki to the grocery and fill the hold with biscuits and salt pork."

Josh was wrong. The next morning was April 21. The sun rose like a coal and during the following week burned like kindling, the temperature climbing into the seventies. Spring came running. The earth swallowed the water, and flowers swam upward into heat and bloom. Bloodroot blossomed in small white puddles, and daffodils filled the dell, turning it into a yellow pool. Purple splattered periwinkle. Blossoms sprayed through Japanese andromeda, the urn-shaped flowers upside down, fragrance trickling from them faint and creamy. Tufts of red and orange suddenly appeared on red maples, almost as if limbs had combed flowers out of light itself. In breezes tags of bark on canoe birch jerked like snags in a low stream. Borers chewed out of dogwood, leaving behind holes covered with flaps that resembled capital D's. Water oozed through the holes in small springs and spreading across the bases of limbs turned them dark and marshy. Earthworms dredged through topsoil and pushed castings to the surface, creating a landscape bumpy with small heaps of moldy slag. Queen bumblebees flew knots just above the ground, hunting nesting sites. A spider inched across the ceiling of Vicki's and my bedroom, its legs moving tentatively like a slow leak.

I spent much of the week walking the woods below the sheep barns. In spring pools wood frogs hatched. The tadpoles hovered loosely together as if they had been riced. In the damp spicebush blossomed in a yellow drizzle. Skunk cabbage thrust green through mud beside spring creeks. At the beginning of the week cabbage leaves clung to each other, humility gluing them together like hands in prayer. By the end of the week leaves unraveled beyond supplication. Spreading luxuriously, the leaves seemed to call attention to themselves, all diffidence vanishing, being a weakness of naive youth. Creeks slipped back between rocks, and marsh marigolds bloomed.

Josh enjoys dampening my enthusiasm for Nature. "Did you," he said, after noticing me leave the woods, "see the acorn in the eye of the squirrel or the capillary in the pupil of the deer tick," this last being a phrase, Josh said, he fashioned "in the twinkling of a chain saw." Spring is the season of the deer tick, and one morning I bagged eight on the front of my sweat pants.

Spring was on the wing as well as in the bud. The slow melody of the mourning dove dripped through mornings. White-throated sparrows called through midday, sounding like water leaking from a kitchen faucet onto a copper sink. Male cowbirds paraded under the bird feeder in the backyard, raising their tails so they resembled spigots, their wings flaring out and down as if they had been switched on. An oriole landed on the feeder. The bird's feathers seemed an emblem of spring itself, the orange on its chest and body rising like water, threatening to sweep over the bird's black head and back. Phoebes perched on saplings, bobbing their tails then splashing into the air after insects. Towhees flickered through briars and fell to the ground, raking their claws backward through litter in search of bugs and seeds. One towhee spent an hour by the back door scratching through husks of sunflowers, in the process digging indentations that resembled impressions of heels. In the woods a pair of ruffed grouse exploded into flight sounding like gusts of air bursting through plugged drain pipes. One morning a red fox stared at me from the edge of a path. In a pasture a killdeer hugged the ground, its head wrinkling black and white. A bluebird clung to the top strand on a barbed wire fence. Suddenly the bird dropped to the ground in an eddy of blue and orange.

Blue azure, cabbage white, and mourning cloak butterflies bubbled through the air. A deer bounded through the woods, its tail shaking like a dustmop. Black racers lay in snarls under plywood beside a field. Ring-necked snakes glistened under rocky till at the foot of a sand pit. Eliza likes snakes, and I took a ringneck home to show her. She named it Simon and dropped it down her shirt. Afterward I returned the snake to the pit. I carried the snake in a Styrofoam cup with a plastic top. The cup once contained night crawlers. Printed on the lid of the cup was "N. C." A fisherman tossed the cup into a patch of swamp dogwood beside the Fenton River. Unlike fishermen who discarded things in the spring, I accumulated. As I tramped across field and wood, I absorbed season, a leaf of Dutchman's breeches waving green through vision like seaweed, rue anemones delicate as star fish, then violets floating through grass and being swept across yards in blue and white flecks. Penny and George accompanied me on walks, and they, too, absorbed the season. The dogs' interests were not quite so elevated as mine, however, and they did not absorb blossoms, but matters closer to roots. They rubbed winter out of their systems and rolled through droppings, the fresher and more fragrant the better.

The past lurks in the present. On a small hill stood the remnants of spreading dogbane. Winter broke many of the plants, but at the top of stems still standing follicles draped like feathers. While the outsides of the follicles were gray and splotched with silver, the insides were beige and shellacked. The follicles themselves twisted slowly through S's, and their inner surfaces reminded me of the streambeds of late summer, dry but flowing smooth with stones. One afternoon after I returned from a walk, a friend telephoned and asked if I would be interested in a post in Richmond. As a boy I spent summers on my grandfather's farm outside Richmond, and suddenly my thoughts jumped out of the present and April and landed in a July forty-seven years ago, in a time when June bugs resembled emeralds and among people who called cicadas, locusts, and dragonflies, snake doctors.

As spring ran through the end of April like a stream, so watery matters coursed through Eliza's mind. On the floor in the upstairs hall I found a pink slip of paper torn from a spiral notebook. Printed on the paper were the first rapids of a story. "The waves," I read, "rocked her bruised body gently. Side to side and back and forth she drifted in the almost never-ending sea. The only thing that kept her above a watery grave was a wooden pole tied to her hands with a coarse rope. All around her wreckage was scattered like chicken feed in a barnyard. A plank here, a plank there, wooden barrels bobbing on the sea as if they had all the time in the world on their hands. All of these were visible in the setting sun, but she did not see them. Her eyes were blind to everything but darkness—pitch-black darkness." Eliza did not complete the story. "Spring is here," she said. "Baseball and soccer have begun, and I don't have time to finish the tale."

Eliza's explanation was reasonable. I spent much of winter inside. Some days I stayed in the house and concocted stories. Other days I sauntered through books in the library, searching for old tales I could adapt to my essays. In spring stories drift from my writing like leaves blown from trees in the fall. Most of my stories take place in Carthage, Tennessee. At the end of April Carthage was quiet. Slubey Garts opened another business, the *Almost Home Photography Emporium,* specializing in pictures of, as Proverbs Goforth put it, "dead corpses." Along with the Tabernacle of Love and the Pillow of Heaven Cemetery, Slubey owned the Haskins Funeral Home. To sweeten burial packages, he hired Isom Legg to take pictures of "dearly beloveds" as they dozed in caskets. An expert painter of barns, Isom knew little about photography, and the first time he took a picture of a body was unfortunate. The camera exploded and set Micah Clemmer's beard on fire. Micah had not shaved in fifty-six years. His beard was so long that Slubey curled it around his neck in a ruffle. The beard flashed into flame. Although Isom quickly dumped a bucket of water into the coffin, the fire singed Micah's face, blackening his skin. Blisters puckered out on Micah's lips. To control swelling Slubey slathered Micah's lips with zinc oxide, turning them white, making the corpse resemble a character in a minstrel show. Even though Micah's grandfather had been a peddler, the Clemmers took great pride in their ancestry. They considered themselves the first family in Horseshoe Bend, and Micah named his farm Palmyra. "The Clemmers go back some way," Turlow Gutheridge said after he saw the corpse, "but old Micah is certainly the most extinguished member of the family."

Aside from Turlow, no one in Carthage believed Slubey could fashion an explanation for the accident that would satisfy Elva,

Micah's widow. The townspeople underestimated Slubey. Micah's name, Slubey told Elva, was "engraved in the *Book of His Blood.*" When Micah descended into the nether region, Satan took one look at him and "belched him from the burning pit," the flames "tinting" Micah's face so that transgressors would see their futures and arm themselves against "Hell's fiery darts." "Soon," Slubey said, dropping a handkerchief dusty with baking soda over the corpse's face, "Micah will shed the dark robe of flesh and don the mantle of everlasting light." In the funeral sermon Slubey urged listeners to heed the Gospel Trumpet. "Look at Micah," he said, "and yield yourself to Jesus. Break the chains of sin and become links in the chain of song." "Slubey was swimming in the Jordan today," Loppie Groat said to Googoo Hooberry after the funeral, "but I have a question about that 'weeping and gnashing of teeth.' Suppose a fellow is old when he dies and don't have no teeth. What does he gnash?" For a moment Googoo was silent. Then gathering his molars and bicuspids, he spoke. "Old folks who don't own false teeth that fit," he said, "gnash their toes."

A joyous continuance runs from one spring to the next, and maybe through life itself. At the end of April Kevin came to my office. I taught Kevin during the fall. For a month and a half Kevin grew a beard. Early in November, he shaved, not, however, his whole face, but only the left side and his right lip, leaving half a goatee jutting out from the right edge of his chin. "I have two photographs to show you," Kevin said, sitting down. In color the first picture showed Kevin and his goatee. The second picture was old and in black and white. A boy about Kevin's age stood in the picture. He was clean-shaven except for a half a mustache on the right side of his upper lip. "That's my father when he was in college," Kevin said, pointing at the snapshot. "After I showed him the photograph of me, he said, 'wait a minute.'" Kevin's father fetched the snapshot from an album in the attic. Kevin had never seen the picture before. "Like father, like son," Kevin said; "things don't change. I guess that's nice." "Yes," I said, "that's very nice."

Things, the seasons themselves, vanish for a time, but then they reappear golden with bloom and similarity. Occasionally I think Tennessee has dropped from my life. Aside from the stories I slap together, Tennessee often seems drier than trees during winter. But as spring turned sugar maples yellow in April, so the past burst blossoming into the present, and I received a bouquet from the real Carthage. Houston McGinness, who knew my grandparents and my father and uncle, sent a letter blooming with anecdotes. One spring day my grandmother showed Mr. McGinness a nest of baby cardinals in a vine outside her kitchen window. "Those were the first baby birds I ever saw," Mr. McGinness wrote, "and probably contributed to my favorite hobby, birdwatching." Unlike classmates in the elementary school, father and Uncle Coleman wore "proper clothes to the school—short pants, stockings held up by fasteners on the underwear, middies, and billed caps." "Once I got to the third grade," Mr. McGinness said, "Mother said it was time for knickers, just like the Pickering boys had worn." Not until the eighth grade did Mr. McGinness wear long trousers. "But," he added, "I never held your father or Coleman responsible for my sartorial suffering, thinking that they, too, perhaps had been uncomfortable."

Seventy-seven years old, Mr. McGinness had recently returned to Carthage after living fifty-two years in California. The return awoke dormant memory, and it rose like sap. Memory brings not simply understanding of the past but also that higher thing, enjoyment of the present. Father and Uncle Coleman spoke impeccable English. "Mother often pointed out that Samuel and

Coleman never used slang or bad grammar," Mr. McGinness said, recounting that he was urged to copy "the speech of the Pickering boys." Father was bookish but not scientific. From Father Mr. McGinness borrowed books by Ernest Thompson Seton, among others, *Rolf in the Woods* and *Wild Animals at Home.* When Mr. McGinness was twelve, Grandmother gave him Father's chemistry set, "an elaborate set containing many chemicals in wood pill boxes and glass vials, all packed together with sundry apparatuses in a beautiful wooden box—very little of the chemicals used."

Thoughts and feelings don't spring up spontaneously in the wild. The roots of my April took seed in the past. After reading the letter, I heard Father's dog Jerry bark in the woods. An Airedale, Jerry rode on the running board of Grandfather's car. "Once," I read, "Jerry tangled with Jimmy Fisher's dog, Jack, a shepherd, and whipped him. Many times afterward, Jimmy said, 'that damn Airedale can whip any dog in town.'" Spring gentles people. In spring people anticipate change and in looking at the natural world momentarily forget self. Coleman has aged beyond competence, and for a year I have managed his life. The only recompense I want—his thanks—he is unable to give. Over the months Coleman has drifted out of quickness into an irritating abstraction. Or at least he was an abstraction until Mr. McGinness's letter arrived and warmed my heart. Coleman ran track at Vanderbilt. "Seeing his name in the sports section of the *Nashville Banner*," Mr. McGinness wrote, "gave me a good feeling. I said to myself, 'I know Coleman.'" The letter helped me to know Coleman, too. I learned that Coleman played on a local semi-professional basketball team, the Carthage Burleys. "He was a guard and the fastest and quickest player." In 1932 the McGinness family built a tennis court below their garden. Coleman and Mr. McGinness played together, the ball bouncing as much through story as it did across line and net into hydrangea. "One summer day Coleman and I were playing," Mr. McGinness recalled, "when Mother came out to the court. She told us we had to stop playing because Mr. Bramlett who lived diagonally across Main Street had just shot himself. Such were the customs in those years."

I answered the letter and sent Mr. McGinness a copy of *Walkabout Year,* my most recent book. In my reply I said that despite my family's having lived in Carthage for three generations, the town that appeared in my books was a fictional place, adding that I hoped the silly behavior of my characters had not offended anyone. Mr. McGinness answered my letter and described a recent trip. "Late yesterday," he wrote, "I drove to Cookville. On the way home I became thirsty and reached for the canteen which I kept on the back seat. Unfortunately the canteen was empty. Although I was almost home, I was so thirsty that I stopped at a little café in South Carthage and ordered a Coca-Cola. As I sat sipping my drink, I heard the waitress say, 'More coffee, Turlow?' Since Turlow is not a common name, I wondered if the man was your friend. About that time another fellow entered the café and spoke to Turlow. 'Turlow,' he said, 'did you hear about Hink Ruunt's fooling with a horse?' Some other man two stools away asked, 'Was it a mare or a stallion?' 'It would be a mare all right,' Turlow said, 'ain't nothing wrong with old Hink.'" "You can see, Sam," Mr. McGinness said, "that your friends are still here in Carthage, and I hope to meet some more of them soon." The letter made me laugh aloud. "What are you laughing at?" Vicki shouted from the kitchen. "I'm laughing at spring," I said, "this joyous, wonderful spring."

WOOD THRUSH

"You would have a big influence on young people," the man said over the telephone, adding, "not many middle-aged people have the chance for a new career." Although drab, my present career was all right, pleasing immodest moments occurring frequently enough to keep lean self-knowledge from the study. "How gratifying it must be," a woman wrote in March, "to see scores of writers copying your essays. I have no influence at all. Last weekend my husband bought a new car. He asked me what color I wanted. I said that I preferred light blue, but that I would settle for red or yellow, anything bright. On Friday he drove home in a black Ford." Recently the word *influence* has spread through my days like hawkweed. Of course *influence* is a seasonal word. As flowers bloom, the gardener's mind runs to cause and effect, recalling fertilizer spread in the fall. In winter people spend long hours inside houses. In spring people roam yards, and sights outside nurture thoughts inside. As bone meal stiffens daffodils, people transplant observation and imagine influence sprouting succulent across mental landscapes.

The influence of literature or education upon people is not so clear as that of manure upon periwinkle. I would have to hoe gardens of essayists before I turned over a writer influenced by my books. As for the young people mentioned on the telephone, hormones, not words, determine their behaviors, root and flower. Tracing literary influence is especially difficult. Shortly after buying WGOD, Slubey Garts decided to build a religious theme park in Carthage. Although small and short-lived, the park may have exerted great influence, affecting one man's writing and through him indirectly determining the course of southern literature in the twentieth century. Built at the end of Tobacco Road in South Carthage, the park was called God's Little Acre. One of the first children to visit the park was Erskine Caldwell, who was spending the summer with a cousin in Gordonsville. Caldwell eventually became a novelist, his two most famous books being *Tobacco Road* and *God's Little Acre*. "Two generations of sociologists," Professor George C. Racker of Harvard University wrote, read the books, "not as fiction but as texts exposing not simply the mind but the body of the South." Perhaps even more profound was the influence of the novels upon literature. "The success of the books," Racker declared, "created a demand for regional fiction peopled by grotesques, a demand which Southern writers rushed to fill, in the process convincing Americans, including Southerners themselves, that the South was a vast desert inhabited by pinworms and polecats." The impression Carthage made upon Caldwell did not extend beyond title. No Jeeter or Ty Ty lived in Smith County, albeit Turlow Gutheridge said that Pluto Swint's belly shook an awful lot like that of Hink Ruunt, "particularly when Hink was hustling about and up to something."

God's Little Acre stayed open for thirty-eight months. Slubey converted a small barn into a museum. The exhibits were all biblical, among other things, a bucket of cicada shells representing the plague of locusts; two stuffed crows, "cousins of the ravens that supplied Elijah with bread and meat," and a millstone, a hunk hammered out of one side so the stone would resemble the one dropped on the head of Abimelech. Atop the stone stood Jacob's ladder, all the rungs painted silver. Just beyond the gate of the park a creek ran down Battery Hill to the Cumberland River. Slubey plugged the stream, and after digging a new channel that curved through the park, named the stream Jordan. He also dug a pond in a corner of the park. Along the shore of the pond, he planted bulrushes. Amid the rushes he anchored a cradle shaped like a small ark. In the cradle he placed a doll. In big gold letters Isom Legg painted "Mozzis" on the doll's forehead.

The most impressive exhibit in God's Little Acre was a wooden whale, "just like," Proverbs Goforth said, "the Leviathan that swallowed Jonah." Beached on the slope below the pond, the Leviathan was eight feet tall and fifteen feet long. While the outside of the fish was black, the inside was painted red and yellow to resemble flames. Six two-by-fours kept the creature's jaws pried apart, and by stepping carefully over the fish's teeth, visitors to the park could enter the whale's belly. Slubey placed benches inside the whale so that Christians could sit and "thinking about Jesus could pound their thoughts into Heavenly Bread." To make the whale's stomach seem real, twice a month Isom Legg scattered catfish entrails under the benches. The best bait doesn't always bring the fish to the hook. Instead of encouraging people to anchor themselves in the shade and replenish their thirst in the living stream, the entrails drove pilgrims grimacing into the wilderness of Smith County. The only person who could endure the fragrance was Cetus Blodgett. Cetus's sense of smell had long fallen martyr to alcohol, and he often spent days in the Leviathan sleeping off the inspirational effects of spirits distilled by Dapper Tuttlebee in Long Dog Hollow.

God's Little Acre came to a stormy end. Changing the course of a creek is harder than convincing a prodigal to yield himself to Jesus. Heavy snow fell during the park's third winter. Melting in a hot flush, the snow roiled down Battery Hill, pushing logs and dirt ahead of it. The Jordan flooded, and water churned through the park, brushing aside the earth dam at the lower end of the pond. Knocked from its moorings, Leviathan swam across the lowlands and plunged into the Cumberland River. When the flood burst through the park, Cetus was sleeping in the whale. He awoke, as he later put it, "in the midst of affliction's black torrent." A log bumped the side of the whale, and "right then and there," Cetus recounted, "I let Jesus into my heart." Near Rome's Ferry the whale slammed against a mudbank, pitching Cetus through its mouth onto land. "The breast of the comforter," Cetus called the shore. From that moment on, Cetus walked in the light, spiritual as well as financial. He wandered the South visiting Pentecostal churches, testifying how the Fisher of Men lifted a sinner from the raging flood and set him down at the Welcome Table. Cetus carried a basket of gourds with him on his travels. On the side of each gourd he carved a whale. After testifying at a meeting, Cetus sold the gourds, autographing each with the name *Jonah*.

The sandbar ripped the bottom out of Leviathan, and the fish turned belly up somewhere below Rome's Ferry. A week later idlers spent a day grappling for the carcass. They did not find it, however. "Five hundred years from now anthropologists will discover it," Turlow Gutheridge said. "After raising it, they will argue over whether it was a boat or a god worshipped by primitive Tennesseans. No matter the debate's resolution, the fish will be put in a museum, and people will travel across the country to see it and Cetus's whiskey jugs, which will also cause argument, one professor declaring them amphora, another maintaining them to be incense pots."

If influencing people, young or old, seemed chancy, changing careers, and thus my writing, had some appeal. When I told Vicki about the whale, she walked out of the room, saying, "I haven't got the energy to listen to a string of fish stories." "Well," I said, "the husband of one of my characters died suddenly last week. Later, his wife told a friend, 'Ober was a corpse just as soon as he died, and I didn't get a chance to say good-bye.'" "What was the woman's name?" Vicki said, pausing in the doorway. "Mrs. Possumly," I said. "Why do you descend so far into Hickdom?" Vicki asked. "When we were first married, you laughed at my jokes," I said. "I may have laughed back then," Vicki said, turning to walk down the hall, "but now is where our paths part." Vicki vanished before I could tell her about Humphries the bullfrog who thought he was an owl and hooted and caught mice every night.

In a tramp through woods Vicki and I might hop over different ends of a log, but our ways rarely part for more than a step or two. Still, Vicki's father taught English at Princeton for thirty years. He believed that an almost regal beauty shimmered from words well-chosen. For him writing was a matter of high seriousness. I agree with Vicki's father. To reach elevated ground, however, I slog through marshes, something that, in truth, I enjoy. My mucky literary doings don't appeal to Vicki, and corny stories that furnish satisfying matter on which I can shake salt and spread butter simply stick between her teeth and, as Loppie Groat might put it, "envelop her in a tornado of vexations."

The morning after receiving the telephone call, I started picking up sticks in the yard. I didn't finish the chore. Spring distracted me. A mockingbird turned musical cartwheels in a dogwood. By the woodpile two flickers hunted ants. Red-backed salamanders lounged under logs, most gray and speckled with blue. Termites unwound annual rings so that a stump slipped and spilled grainy and red along a path. Ground ivy climbed one side of the stump. Resembling flecks of sky, blossoms whorled around stems. Stamens pinched together against the upper lip of the corolla, forming an hourglass of white vapor. While I looked at ivy, a garter snake slipped across the path. I moved, and the snake pulled itself into leaves under an oak, the rings around its eyes glinting gold and fresh. From a black birch catkins glowed like strings of coals. Blossoms splattered Norway maples, from a distance resembling dabs of yellow paint. At the center of the flowers lay shallow cups overflowing with green wax. Near a spring pool northern white violets bloomed. Smaller than other white violets, the flowers hugged the ground. Green trickled down the upper two petals of the blossoms while purple veins ran damp through central lower petals.

A new career meant forsaking the familiar. Loss would accompany gain. For me success has usually depended upon inner, not outer, matters, learning to appreciate the tangible and immediate instead of imagining an abstraction like influence. Besides, I thought, kneeling over the violets, place itself changed. While retaining enough of the familiar to make one comfortable, change shimmered with the seasons, enabling one to see and delight in difference.

The campus was bright with spring. Grading final essays and thinking about careers, I'd hardly noticed it. Many people, I thought, would welcome an opportunity to change careers, particularly if the new post seemed prestigious. Suddenly I remembered something Slubey Garts said in a sermon. "The live fish swims against the stream." I pushed career out of mind and walked across the campus. Gallery pear, silverbell, lilac, Oriental cherry, and shadbush were blooming. Red oaks shed catkins, and the ground under the trees buckled like thick carpet. Petals peeled from saucer magnolia and lay beneath trees in brown slices. From Washington hawthorn petals fell in a pink flurry.

Five sharp sepals formed the calyxes, and after petals tumbled away, turned limbs into constellations of green stars, anthers spraying from them like solar flares. Flowers from Japanese maple tumbled on a picnic table behind the Life Sciences Building. Drying, the flowers curled inward and granular, and I mistook them for caterpillar droppings. In damp shadows below the building, bleeding heart, jack-in-the-pulpit, mayapple, and columbine bloomed.

Flowers on columbine were dark blue, and their symmetry almost seduced me into believing the comforting old sentimentality that a creator designed the world. Perhaps, I pondered, my skepticism of a Great First Cause undermined the lure of a new career. For me career seemed artificial and designed. Life was not something shaped or controlled but happenings that one learned to enjoy or at least to cope with. Instead of a climb up a narrow path toward a goal, life ought to be a ramble in which distraction provided the stuff of joy. Rarely, of course, are people apologists for anything greater than their own inclinations. Not surprisingly my musings not only justified my meanderings but elevated them almost to the ideal. Happily, however, before I turned my doings into pages of a self-help book, distraction saved me, and I was on the ground examining blossoms on mayapple. The petals glistened like wax paper at the bottom of a cake pan. Amid the paper lay stamens resembling loaves of bread sliced in half and buttered, not in the centers, however, but along edges. A young rabbit noticed me and hopped out of a patch of wake-robin. Students abandon cats on the campus, and the rabbit stood little chance of growing into an adult. If I caught the rabbit and raised him at home, later, I thought, I could free him in the raspberry patch by the Fenton River where he might survive longer. As I stepped toward the rabbit, a wood thrush flew into a dawn redwood. I had not seen a wood thrush so early in May, so I watched him, hoping he would sing. After preening for a moment, the thrush darted away, and when I turned back toward the building the rabbit was gone.

On several trees buds were still firm: black tupelo, lacebark elm, and Kentucky coffee tree, among others. Buds on fern leaf beech had begun unraveling into bronze while leaves on castor aralia exploded in puffs, resembling tissue paper being pulled through narrow openings. New leaves of Korean Stewardia splayed upward, usually in clusters of four, resembling green candle holders. On sweet buckeye sepals rolled backward, reminding me of wrapping paper torn from a present by an impatient child. From yellowwood leaflets dangled in sevens shining so brightly they looked as if they had been washed in a silver rain. Flower buds on yellowwood had not stretched into lazy panicles but clung together in knobby bundles. On London plane tree fruits were small. Just beginning to unwind along stems, they had not rolled through season absorbing size.

I ambled from one tree to another. Students began examinations within a week, and to set an industrious example, I pretended purpose determined the course of my wanderings. On elms samaras sprouted from twigs in thick bunches resembling cabbage leaves. On slippery elms I counted the number of samaras in a bunch. I examined three batches; the first contained twenty samaras, the other two fifteen samaras apiece. "What are you doing?" a student said, seeing me writing in my notebook. "Studying fertility," I said, adding, "I am curious about the effect of gasoline fumes upon seed germination." "Cool," the student said as I thumbed a fourth batch of seeds. This time I counted twenty-seven samaras. In trying to appear analytical, I may have lumped together two batches of seeds that grew side by side. Mistake does not deter the true scientist, though, and I soon forgot the count. On a Siberian elm I counted two batches of samaras, the first consisting of eight seeds, the second of eleven. On a camperdown elm I counted only one batch containing thirty-six seeds. Beginning counting is easy; stopping is difficult. The previous Saturday students played oozeball in the field near the Fine Arts Building. Oozeball is mud volleyball and ruins clothes. At the end of the day many students abandoned their shoes, and while walking home, I counted forty-one shoes stuck in the ground.

"Are you really interested in a different job?" Vicki asked that evening. "You are always writing that you have aged beyond ambition." "I don't think I am interested," I said, "but I'll decide tomorrow." "Don't forget what Slubey Garts said," Vicki replied. "The man who sits on the floor doesn't worry about falling." The next morning I did not think about career. Unlike Edward and Eliza, Francis did not participate in sports in elementary school. Francis inherited my athletic ability and cannot throw or catch a ball. This past fall when he started high school I urged him to try out for crew. I told him that if he disliked rowing he could stop after two weeks, adding that when he applied to college he would need something other than straight A's on his transcript. Despite all my palaver about the insignificance of career and ambition, I want good things for my children, though like many parents I am not sure what the good things of life really are. In private I suspect that college shapes conformists, people whose visions are so narrowed by education that they don't notice much that passes before them. Nevertheless, since I cannot define the good things, much less explain how a person achieves them, I urge conventional behavior upon my children. Sports have changed since I was young, and although I believe that sports now undermine virtue, I encourage the children to participate. Last week Edward's baseball team played a school from Hebron. A batter from Hebron hit a slow ground ball to the Mansfield shortstop. The play at first was close, but the shortstop threw the runner out. The only umpire stood behind home plate. As the runner crossed the base, he jerked the first baseman off the bag, grabbing the boy's shirt with his left hand so that the umpire would not see. Everyone, including the umpire, saw the runner's action. The umpire shouted, but the boy's coach only smiled. "You do anything you can to win," a father standing next to me said, shaking his head, "even in eighth grade."

Despite the muddiness of my motivation, Francis enjoyed rowing, and so instead of deciding whether to embark on a new career, I drove to Simsbury to watch Francis row. I went with my friend Neil. While Francis rowed four in the second boat, Neil's son Dan rowed bow in the first boat. West of the Connecticut River, Simsbury was a rowing town. Envious rumor declared that the Simsbury boathouse held more than twenty boats. "We need to make a showing," Neil said. "My appearance will stun Francis," I said. "I have never seen him play a sport." The boys rowed on the Farmington River. Observers stood on a bridge that had recently been restored. I walked from one side of the bridge to the other, just to say that I had crossed the mighty Farmington. Constructed in 1892, the bridge resembled a railway bridge. I asked nine people if the bridge was originally built for trains. No one knew. Girders on the bridge had been painted green. Attached to a girder above the walkway at each end of the bridge was a metal marker. Stamped on the marker and painted yellow were the names of the selectmen who authorized construction of the bridge in 1892, W. H. Whitehead, Harvey Tucker, and G. B. Holcomb.

The river was narrow, and grackles flew rattling from one side to the other. Simsbury supporters crowded the bridge. Three adults wore sweat shirts with "Habitat for Humanity" printed on the fronts, individual letters of the words composed of stick people cavorting like gymnasts. On the front of a sweat shirt worn by a high school student was the word "SIMSBURY," under which appeared a small building and the inscription "Best Little Oarhouse in Connecticut." When Francis's crew rowed under the bridge toward the starting line, a Simsbury girl exclaimed, "Oh, he's so cute." "Some nice things never change," Neil said. In part continuance lay behind the appeal of rowing. I rowed for my college at Cambridge, and when Francis's boat churned back under the bridge during the race, I saw, if not myself, at least a link between generations. Each summer the boys attend Camp Timanous in Maine. In the 1960s I was a counselor at Timanous. At the end of camp Vicki and I take the children to Nova Scotia, and we stay two or so weeks in the house in which Vicki spent summers as a child. Such things will not unwind the dizzying spin of change. They do, however, bind past to present, and maybe by awakening the children to continuance and community make them aware of place, landscapes bushy not only with tradition and story but also with trees and flowers, Solomon's seal and box elder, sweetgum and wild strawberry.

From Simsbury I rushed back to the middle school and watched Edward roam centerfield for two innings. Afterward I attended the Spring Band Concert in the school auditorium. Eliza played clarinet in the Junior Band. That night a wood thrush sang from the woods behind the house. I listened until the music stopped. Then I wrote a letter declining the new career. In the letter I described my day and to the puzzlement of my correspondent, wisteria blooming on campus. "Well, Mr. Perfect," Vicki said when I came to bed, "what did you decide to do?" Vicki occasionally dubs me Mr. Perfect. I prefer to think the phrase a compliment or a term of endearment, though, to be honest, I suspect that Vicki would not accept either interpretation.

Rain started that night, and the next morning was wood thrush weather. Following an abandoned road, I walked down through the woods behind the sheep barns. Garlic mustard and winter cress bloomed in a wet field. Under trees rue and wood anemone, dwarf ginseng, downy yellow violet, and small-flowered crow-foot blossomed. Deer bobbed slowly between pines softening the rocky hillside. Yellow seeped through the bark of sweet birch, and the fragrance of spicebush rinsed the air. Raindrops fell like buds into the beaver pond, where they rippled into flowers. I sat on a rock heaved from a stone wall by frost and listened to wood thrushes. They called from damp lowlands. Their songs rang like liquid color, bending blue through trees like stained glass. A Canada goose beat its way over a ridge honking mournfully, making me glad I was sitting on a rock. Ralph Waldo Emerson urged readers to hitch their wagons to stars. If Emerson had listened closely to the wood thrush, he would have told people to hitch their stars to wagons.

SATISFACTION

"I want to live life to the fullest," the man said. "How can I make every moment meaningful? How can I be satisfied?" A stranger, the man telephoned at 8:30 in the evening. He called from Atlantic City, a town that panders to dissatisfaction. "Atlantic City," my friend Josh said, "the City of Dreams, most of which turn to sand and roulette." Although I stumbled through a paragraph, I didn't answer the man's questions. Instead of enriching days, meaning reduces, forcing happening into significance. Even asking if one is satisfied leads to dissatisfaction. Moreover, escaping malaise is difficult in a materialistic, goal-oriented society in which a person is measured by possessions. Perhaps the attempt to quantify the intangible, the use of words such as *measure* and *weigh*, contributes to melancholy. If people stopped setting goals, maybe they would enjoy life more. As soon as a child kicks diapers aside and totters into the sunny yard of life, counselors begin blowing like clouds across the heavens, darkening pleasure by asking, "What do you want to be?" When I was young, no one asked me such questions. Indeed no one has ever addressed that question to me. As I had no goals at ten, so I have none at fifty-five. Because I did not set goals, neither failure nor success has thrilled or disappointed me.

Instead of living a life throbbing with meaning, I have just lived. The day on which the man called was full. At eight-thirty Donna cleaned my teeth. Afterward I visited with Ellen and Roger at the Cup of Sun for twenty minutes. At ten o'clock George cut my hair. At eleven I went to the gymnasium and swam two kilometers. Early in the afternoon I mowed the yard. At five o'clock Edward finished baseball practice, and I fetched him from the middle school. From six to seven-thirty Eliza practiced soccer at Spring Hill, and I dropped her off and picked her up. The doings of a day are too frail and too strong to withstand dissection. A pop anatomologist could, I am sure, slice through life with a hammer, pounding hours and pleasure into razzleum-dazzleum absurdity. "There is a slight stretching of the onolas cellusis," an analysis might begin, "complicated by a chronnecrosis of the lamifuresis, resulting in some denusion of the malparium, in other words, to be plain, a blepharmedia multipediti marginallis."

For the two days following the telephone call I gave examinations at eight o'clock in the morning. Although not the stuff of dissatisfaction, sitting examinations can bore, so I decided to "take inventory," as a student who worked behind stage at the university theater said. Thirty-two students took the first examination, thirteen males and nineteen females. Six students were left-handed, two-thirds of them male. Seven females wore scrunchies. And while eight students wore baseball caps, the number was evenly split between male and female. Only one student, a female, wore a cap backward. Six students wore glasses, three of them sitting in the row of desks next to the window. The day was chilly, and only one boy wore short pants, while a single girl wore a skirt. The skirt was denim. In fact denim was popular as twenty-four students dressed in blue jeans. Eleven students wore sweat shirts. I tried to read inscriptions printed across the chests of the shirts. I was not successful. To read the print I would have been forced to lean over desks, making students behave unnaturally, thereby undermining the integrity of the inventory. Nevertheless I noted "EXP Jeans" stamped in green across the front of a gray sweat shirt. On another sweat shirt Tigger posed atop Winnie the Pooh. Under Pooh appeared a lumpy mound of words. I read the words, in the process unnerving the subject wearing the sweat shirt. "This is so embarrassing," she said. "I fell out of bed this morning and just grabbed clothes." Printed on the shirt was "Tigger chuckled, 'What's a Pooh?' 'You're sitting on one,' Pooh said."

Although the examination took place early in the morning, no student ate in the room. Two males did, however, drink liquids, the first coffee from a gray plastic mug on which was printed "DDS Mug. The Department of Dining Services. I have my DDS mug because it's the only cup that can leave the dining room." The second student sipped Fruitopia, a soda manufactured by Coca-Cola. Containing "10% Fruit Juice," the drink was a blend of water and jiggers of apple, passion fruit, and strawberry juices. Across the front of the label cavorted three plump strawberries, two apples breathless and red, and then a dizzy green swirl resembling a lollipop, this last spinning over a tepid blue sea. The boy did not finish his Fruitopia. "Too sweet," he said, placing the bottle in the waste can, "but this was all I could find before the test." In not purchasing a drink the previous night, the boy was an exception to the general run of students. The rest of the class came to the examination well-prepared. No one borrowed a pen from me, and sticking out of the backpack of another boy was a roll of toilet paper, the wrapping stripped away but the roll itself untouched.

I did not impose meaning upon the inventory. Still, the day was chilly, and temperature, I suspect, was part of the reason just one subject wore a short-sleeved shirt, to be specific, a T-shirt on which a yellow sunflower blossomed above the black earth. The inventory also helped me pass time, and only occasionally did I glance out the window. The sky resembled slate. While buds on a white ash by the parking lot had burst into green, new leaves on the silver maple beside Gilbert Road shook in the breeze like finely cut snowflakes. In part universities exist to ferret out meaning, and so in hopes of reaching conclusions, I repeated some sections of the inventory the following morning. A nap, I am afraid, prevented my being as thorough as I had been the previous day. Nevertheless in a class of thirty-seven students, fifteen of whom were male, I found four left-handed subjects, the number being evenly split between the sexes. Four females wore scrunchies, three of them on the backs of their heads and one on her right wrist. Three females also wore barrettes, this accounting for the difference between the number of scrunchies worn by members of the two classes. Four students wore baseball caps, all girls. Interestingly these four females were the first four students to complete the examination and leave the room. Although no conclusion ought to be teased from the observation, the odds of such an occurrence are one in 66,045, a statistic I find almost satisfying. When set beside this number, other facts pale, even the observation that in this second and larger class, three males rather than two consumed liquids, a fifty percent increase in the number of drinkers, all of them drinking coffee, two from cups with "DUNKIN' DONUTS" printed on them and one from a cup supplied by Lizzie, who operates the snack wagon parked outside the English department.

I doubt the caller from Atlantic City would find the results of my inventory entirely satisfying. Much as my professional career, as social scientists label teaching, has not soldered meaning to my days, so domestic life has not nurtured fulfillment like an aged orange nurtures fungus. Indeed the person who wants romance to generate satisfaction would do well to bypass the altar, hop on the Reading Railroad, and head for St. Charles Place, or if he has a deeper pocket, Ventnor or Pacific Avenue. Last week I received proof sheets for a new collection of essays. "I don't want to read my book," I moaned, thumbing the pages. "Nobody else does either," Vicki answered. Vicki thinks stories should probe truth and explain life. Rarely do tales in my essays mean anything. "Vicki is an idealist," Josh said, "and you are a nihilist. No wonder you get along so well together." Josh may be right. That aside, however, instead of sitting behind a desk pondering significance, lack of fulfillment gnawing at me like hunger, I wander aisles of students counting scrunchies. Often after class I visit Carthage, Tennessee, a town in which stories are rarely reduced to meaning.

Last month the Tabernacle of Love held its annual spring picnic. During the outing children bobbed for apples, an activity later criticized by worshippers at the Church of the Chastening Rod. "Mother Eve was fond of bobbing for apples," Malachi Ramus, a deacon, said, "but instead of angel food she swallowed worm poison." The remark did not bother Slubey Garts, owner and minister of the Tabernacle of Love. "The Ramuses ain't known for brains, but Malachi," Slubey said, "is the most ignorant Ramus of them all."

Six months earlier Slubey might not have swatted Malachi's remark aside so easily. Recently, though, Slubey purchased a radio station, WGOD. The most popular program broadcast by the station was *The Evening Star Gospel and Holiness Hour*, hosted by Slubey himself. The success of the show covered Slubey like fingernail polish, "killing the chiggers of criticism," Proverbs Goforth said, "dead as carp." The highlight of each show was the testimonial of a repentant sinner. Because two people testified, last week was a doubleheader, or an Ahab and Jezebel, as Proverbs phrased it. Jessie Mae Hedges from Vonore described making link sausages from turnips. "I minced a bushel of turnips and poured in red food coloring," she said. "Then I added summer savory, sage, and black pepper. The mixture looked like meat, and I charged top dollar, telling customers I used King Pork in my sausage."

Slubey's second guest was Willie Busler from New Tazewell. For years Willie wrote advertising testimonials for patent medicines, most of which, he said, were "cholera-morbus inducers." Willie read two examples of his work. The first testimonial appeared under the headline "FROM A PROMINENT CLERGY-MAN." "I read about DR. STOBO'S BLUE SUPPOSITORIES in the *Evening Kidney*. For six years my beloved wife Carmentia Magdalen suffered from a wasting disease that baffled the most eminent practitioners of the medical fraternity. Twenty months ago Carmentia passed away. I then suggested to her that since she had little to lose that she might try DR. STOBO'S BLUE SUP-POSITORIES. She quickly consented. After only two weeks of taking the SUPPOSITORIES, Carmentia's complexion improved, her costiveness vanished, and she sat up in her coffin and shouted, 'catterwampus!' She is now hale and hearty. The coffin is in the shed filled with canned snaps and tomatoes, and Carmentia is spending this summer touring the battlefields of the Civil War. I consider the result almost a miracle, and I recommend DR. STOBO'S BLUE SUPPOSITORIES to all husbands afflicted with sickly or dead wives. Rev. Odle W.V. Jarrett, Hunts-ville, Alabama." Supposedly written by Orman Bailey, the mayor of Dewlap, South Carolina, the second testimonial was shorter. Like Carmentia, Orman had lost flesh and health. The suppositories rectified the problem immediately. "I have an appetite like a sawmill and have gained over three hundred pounds in twenty-four hours," Orman reported. "My wife, Nola, has given birth to triplets. The chickens are laying. Lloyd the mule is pregnant, and business at the hardware store has increased seventy-five percent."

"To understand, much less appreciate such stories," Josh said, "requires years of education and takes great spiritual awareness." Josh's comment mystified me. What is clear is that some readers, not Vicki, however, enjoy slipping the leash of high seriousness. Frequently readers write me and describe things my characters have done but which I haven't heard about. "'Did you hear about the big fish Juno Feathers found in her chicken house?' Loppie Groat asked Googoo Hooberry in Ankerrow's Café," a man wrote from Woodbridge last month. "'No,' Googoo said, 'what kind was it?' 'A nice long perch,' Loppie answered."

Surroundings influence behavior. No matter how firmly a person anchors himself in the shallows, a current will eventually drag him toward midstream. I want Vicki to appreciate my writing, and so in hopes of improving the literary content of my stories I sometimes subject myself to a regimen of patented, improving reading. Two weeks ago I read the Riverside Edition of *The Writings of John Burroughs,* ten volumes published in 1895. Burroughs was a famous naturalist, and I read *The Writings* in order to make my descriptions of Nature poetical. I failed. I have aged into feeling diminished when I see a dead squirrel by the roadside. Burroughs admired and studied birds. Birds so intrigued him that he shot almost all he saw, even off their nests. Burroughs's pursuit of knowledge narrowed his vision and, for me, reduced his stature. Markings on the books themselves soon interested me more than Burroughs's learned observations, no matter their caliber. Inscribed on the title page of *Wake-Robin,* the first volume in the set, was "R. E. Dodge from Aunt Harriet and Aunt Mary, Christmas, 1895." On June 19, 1929, Dodge donated the set to the library of "Connecticut Agricultural College." Dodge owned the books for almost thirty-five years, and I wondered if he finally found Burroughs's readiness to kill repulsive. Had Dodge, like me, grown beyond goals that destroy not simply birds, but that, in aiming life like a gun, shrink a person's capacity to appreciate?

I did not spend much time pondering Dodge's motivation. In March Vicki, the children, and I visited Princeton. In the attic Vicki discovered a doll she owned as a child. Eliza named the doll Abigail and brought her back to Storrs. Over the years Abigail's clothes had vanished, and she made the trip clad in a worn shift. The day after I returned *The Writings* to the library, I drove Vicki and Eliza to Wal-Mart to buy the makings of a new wardrobe. Shopping for clothes tires me, and I remained outside the store, sitting on a red bench in an enclosed porch. For a while I watched a man stuff cans into a recycling machine manufactured by Tomra. The man put twenty cans into the machine and received a chit for a dollar. The machine refused to accept one can and a plastic bottle, and the man dumped them into a gray trash barrel. Sitting on the porch was tedious, and I drifted toward the edge of dissatisfaction, once jerking myself back by studying the logo of the Tomra corporation—a blue bottle, from the neck of which three white lines circled the bottle, curving beneath its base then turning upward and ending in an arrow pointing at the other side of the neck. From a distance the logo resembled an eyeball. Because the image in the pupil never changed, I grew tired of staring at it, and for a while I listened to grocery carts jangling as employees fetched them from the parking lot and pushed them through the front door in trains. The longest train consisted of twenty-eight carts. The engineer was a sixteen-year-old boy who took great pride in not losing a single cart to derailment as the train thumped across the porch.

The porch was not a roundhouse of activity. After Vicki and

Eliza had shopped for twenty-five minutes, I became impatient and, standing, peered inside the store. To the right of the door a large bald man with a black mustache sat behind a card table. He was Ox Baker, a retired professional wrestler, "The Ugly Hero," a poster stated. In order to raise money for an employee of Wal-Mart who was in the hospital, Mr. Baker was signing a glossy, eight-by-ten-inch photograph of himself. Ox loomed in the center of the picture, his hands curved like grapples. He did not wear a shirt, and hair rolled across his chest in heavy black waves. Jury-rigged around his left elbow was an elastic bandage. Tubes of tape supported three fingers on his left hand, and resembling a broken spar, a splint was strapped to his thumb. After Ox signed "To Eliza" on a photograph, we chatted. Ox had wrestled in Nashville, and when he mentioned Tex Riley and Jackie Fargo, a train of wrestling associations rattled through my mind—the Hippodrome the first cart, the fairgrounds the second. One night at the Hippodrome I watched the Mighty Jumbo wrestle five midgets. The last time he saw Jumbo, Ox recounted, Jumbo was working in a carnival in Florida. "I am sorry we took so long," Vicki said, suddenly appearing at my side. "I hope you weren't bored." "Not at all," I said, waving good-by to Ox. "We should shop here more often."

The caller from Atlantic City would probably turn down an invitation to sit on the porch outside Wal-Mart. Moreover, I suspect he would think the way I spent Memorial Day weekend remarkably unsatisfactory. Late in May a mallard nested in grass growing against the wall of the building that houses the English department. Secretaries supplied the duck with food and water. "The weekend is long, and I am worried," Helen said. "Since you live close to campus, would you mind feeding the duck? She is going to be a mommy soon." Not only did feedings impose structure on the weekend, but they provided pleasure and knowledge, this last obtained with bread rather than a shotgun. When I first approached the nest, the bird made a panting sound in hopes of frightening me away. Soon, though, the duck ate from my hand. On Saturday I fed her bread baked by a French bakery in Stafford Springs, a place popular with gourmands from Storrs. On Sunday I gave her Pepperidge Farm's Crunchy Grains Bread, made from "Whole Natural Grain." While one piece of the French bread was all the duck wanted, she quickly pecked through two slices of Crunchy Grains, then wagged her bill and begged for more. On Monday the duck celebrated the holiday with her favorite bread, snatching three slices of Arnold's stone ground Sprouted Wheat Bread out of my hand before I could soak them in water.

To put days on a sure thing a person ought to turn away from win and show and leap through place. As one wanders place, questions about meaning and fulfillment fray and slip from consciousness. Last week Eliza played softball at Hampton. The baseball field perches on the lip of a beech wood that slides smoothly into a valley like a cup into a saucer. At the end of the second inning vultures floated up from the valley and over the outfield like grounds swirling in tea. Just before dusk I roamed the wood. Two wood ducks paddled along a creek, and in the soft sun damp new leaves dangled from beeches, yellowing the air. The next morning I explored the university campus. Atop Golf Hill lupin glistened in blue spires. In low shade by the pharmacy building yellow lady's slippers bloomed, the two side petals spinning like halves of a mustache. I examined three flowers; on each blossom the side petals turned through four spirals. Near the Benton Museum red oak saplings poked through lilacs and drained away the sun. I dug two lilac suckers and planted them in the side yard, the first from a plant sudsy with white blossoms, the second from a lilac with purple flowers dark as evening.

Out of a crab apple I sliced a nest of tent caterpillars resembling a sock. To give my rambles the illusion of purpose, I toy with figures. At home I asked the children to guess the number of caterpillars in the nest. Edward guessed sixty-eight, and both Francis and Eliza, seventy-two. The nest contained three hundred and eighty-three caterpillars. Lest I be thought a modern John Burroughs wrecking havoc on the natural creation in the name of curiosity, let me say that I opened the nest near cherry trees bright with new leaves, the caterpillars' favorite munchies.

Years ago when I first explored the campus, flowers absorbed my attention. Now I notice trees. Unlike many flowers that vanish during winter, trees suffer the seasons, almost becoming emblems of endurance, something I admire more as I age and blight affects me trunk and bole. Many trees on campus seem companions, if not of daily life, at least of years. New growth seeped glowing down the branches of Norway spruce. Against a pillow of blue sky Austrian pines bristled like soldiers, old campaigners gray and hardy. In contrast tassels of yellow peas switched lightly on golden chaintrees. A cloud of small bees drifted over English hawthorn, the flowers, pats of white butter, petals melting from them and dripping to ground. Wider than tall, copper beeches loomed like pots in a pantry, one moment bronze and clean, the next purple and charred.

I am a compulsive walker. Once started, I don't stop until I have gamboled away my energy. I spent the next day roaming the university farm. Around the cornfield on Bean Hill highbush cranberry and autumn olive bloomed, white flowers on the olive aging yellow, dappling the edge of the woods. Cherry trees looked as if a steel brush had been rubbed through them, the teeth snagging and pulling crinkles of blossoms from the tips of limbs. Beside a stone wall rose a cushion of rye grass, spikelets shunting in and out of colors, blue, green, yellow, red, and then from flower scales fringes of silver blades. Barn swallows spun over a field, orange and blue streaming from their tails and lingering forked and ghostly in the air.

Under trees in the woods leaves of Canada mayflower jutted from the ground looking like spoons. Near laurel, lady's slippers swelled pink and inflamed. In the Ogushwitz meadow warmth radiated from Indian poke, the six stamens on each blossom resembling fragile yellow hearts. Cedar waxwings skittered through trees by the beaver pond. Along the edge of the pond yellow warblers circled, establishing territories. I followed Kessel Creek and climbed the ridge above the pond. False Solomon's seal bloomed in dirt atop a rock. I sat on the rock and noticed maidenhair and long beech ferns growing above the creek. Small beetles congregated in the flowers of false Solomon's seal, on each shaft a single long-horned beetle, then several brown throscid beetles.

The throscid beetles were minute. Even with a hand lens I could not see them clearly. I needed young eyes. The next day the children walked with me, Edward immediately spotting a ladybug the size of a freckle, then on a tree a jumping spider resembling a fleck of gray lichen. Later in Schoolhouse Brook Francis noticed a crayfish clinging to a stone. As a boy in Virginia I caught buckets of crayfish. I had not seen one in decades. My joints snap and creak when I bend over streams. Moreover, as I drive little at night because headlights weep through my eyes, so the light in creeks blears then staggers across bottoms, making objects drift like water. "How was the stroll?" Vicki asked when we returned home. "I saw a crayfish," I said, "the first since childhood. The day could not have been better. I broke the bank."

OLD HOME

Last spring Uncle Coleman collapsed. In July Vicki and I drove to Houston, and I took over management of his life and placed him in a nursing home. During this past year I wrote Coleman twice a week. Every weekend I telephoned, usually reaching him after a dozen attempts. In March Coleman stopped answering the phone. The first week in June I flew to Texas to visit Coleman. Not sure what to expect, I drove directly from the airport to the nursing home. Heat sagged woolen in the air. Beside roads crape myrtle bloomed, the flowers resembling sleeves of heavy fabric pulled from carpets. Asphalt bubbled in the parking lot outside the nursing home, and great-tailed grackles hissed and whistled, exploding like fireworks. In July when Vicki and I left the home, we noticed an old man sitting in a wheelchair by the door. Perched on his head was a baseball cap, the bill turned slightly to the right. Stamped on the cap was "Green's Bayou Terminal." The man wore white basketball shoes and pulled himself around the home by hooking his heels into rugs. Rarely did the man stop singing. Stephen Foster's songs were his favorites, and as we left the building, he was singing "My Old Kentucky Home." "Along the mundanious shores of mortality," as Proverbs Goforth put it, "change is slow." When I walked into the home, I saw the man sitting in his wheelchair. He wore basketball shoes and the baseball cap, and he was singing "My Old Kentucky Home."

I stayed four nights in Houston, all in a motel three and a half miles from the home. My room had two double beds, three locks on the door, and an alarm clock I couldn't set. The motel provided a small breakfast, and each morning I ate cornflakes and drank coffee, both from Styrofoam cups. Every day I made four trips to the home, staying an hour and sometimes two hours each time. I went after breakfast, just before lunch, early in the afternoon, and then after dinner. I ate one full meal a day, always in a Vietnamese restaurant. At night I tried to read a book on gardening, but my interest wilted, and I watched television. I never saw an entire program. Instead I surfed channels, *Star Trek* splashing up here, professional basketball washing ashore there. When I was not at the home, I trudged across concrete pans outside shopping centers. I bought Coleman a hair brush, six pairs of gray socks, three striped polo shirts, and two pairs of trousers with elastic waistbands.

Vicki instructed me to mark clothes with a "Rub-a-Dub" laundry pen, saying, "No other brand will do." In H-E-B Pantry Foods, the eighth store I visited, I found the pen. One of Coleman's childhood nicknames was Candy Hound, and in Kroger I bought him eight pounds of Russell Stover's Assorted Creams. Cardigan sweaters are easy to slip on old people, and I roamed malls searching for one. I tried Sears, Old Navy, Venture, Wal-Mart, Target, Marshall's, Ross, J. C. Penney's, Foley's, Gap, Zak's, Structure, Dillard's, Palais Royal, T. J. Maxx, Abercrombie and Fitch, and Mervyn's of California. No store stocked cardigans, and exasperation caused me to overheat. "I am frozen," I said to a clerk near the end of my search. "How can you stand Houston? The city is an iceberg. I've got to have a cardigan. If I don't find one soon,

I'm going to move north where the temperature is warmer." Occasionally I took a break from the search. One afternoon I went into a Barnes and Noble to see how many of my books the store had in stock. I didn't find any. In a parking lot I noticed two cars with the same vanity plate, a spin-off from Pennsylvania's motto, "You've Got a Friend in Pennsylvania." Stamped on the plate was "Texas—You've Got a Friend in Jesus." Printed in the upper left corner of the plate was "Never Expires." In the upper right corner appeared "John 15: 13–15." I read the verses in the Gideon Bible in my room. The thirteenth verse was familiar: "Greater love hath no man than this, that a man lay down his life for his friends."

Before moving into the home Coleman lived in his bedroom for four years. He left bed only to eat or go to the lavatory. Once in the nursing home, he stopped walking. Staff tried to rouse him, dressing him and sitting him in a wheelchair. As soon as Coleman was in the chair, however, he slumped over and slept, looking as if he were melting out of time. A year ago Coleman was almost blind. In hopes of improving his sight I arranged a cataract operation. The operation failed. When I arrived, his left eye was swollen. I asked him if the eye hurt. "I hope it doesn't hurt," he answered, adding, "how long have you had this eye trouble?" I asked Coleman scores of questions in hopes of startling him into alertness. On the first day of my visit, he answered me occasionally. Later he refused to respond unless I fed him candy. "I am glad in many ways that my mother's not here, my daddy, too," he said one night. "I'd be a lot of trouble to them." When I mentioned his wife, Amanda, he said, "well, there wasn't anything around Carthage to marry." After a pause he added, "I guess they thought the same about me." Amid the dross of hours, frail slivers of memory glittered. "Daddy," Coleman said, "didn't know anything about mechanics. He didn't pay attention to that." Although Grandfather sold insurance, he couldn't drive, and a man called Monk drove him around Carthage. On his travels Grandfather boarded with farmers, staying up late at night, Coleman said, "telling big stories."

In my books Carthage is a fictional place. Nevertheless, a real town exists. Pickerings lived there for three generations, and I mentioned Carthage often in hopes of awakening recollection. "I remember something about Carthage," he said one afternoon. Memory progressed no further. Coleman's next sentence was, "This is awfully good candy." That night Coleman described the "Carthage Ready Band." Consisting of eight or so men playing the bass horn, saxophone, clarinet, trombone, and trumpet, the band performed at funerals. When Coleman mentioned the band, I immediately thought of my fictional town. I decided that Slubey Garts should sell a band option as part of the burial package at Haskins Funeral Home. Slubey sent Proverbs Goforth to Nashville to purchase second-hand uniforms. Proverbs bought a rack of uniforms worn by high school bands. Because the outfits came in a rainbow of colors, blue and white for Litton, gray and red for East, for example, Slubey decided that the name of the band ought to refer to Joseph's coat of many colors. "Slubey is always marching in the shining way, finding new ways to broadcast the blessed story," Proverbs said. Slubey did not fumigate the uniforms or patch the name into existence, because I suddenly heard strains of "Softly and Tenderly." As I listened to the words and looked at Coleman, his white hair spilling across a pillow, I felt both sad and happy. "Softly and tenderly Jesus is calling, calling for you and for me," the hymn stated, the phrase "come home" glowing through the refrain like a sunset.

Among old people in the home conversation started and ended abruptly. One morning a man suddenly jerked straight in a wheelchair and, staring at a woman a yard away, shouted, "Put some clothes on her!" People at Coleman's table in the dining room could not feed themselves. The man sitting next to Coleman babbled, using syllables more than words. Only once did I hear him say a sentence. On Sunday his wife visited and fed him. He didn't recognize her. Halfway through the meal, he turned to her and said reassuringly, "You've a good chance of getting married." I fed Coleman. He had lost the lower half of his false teeth, having, so far as I could diagnose, two uppers. As a result, his meals were pureed. "Eating this way is easier for him," a nurse told me. "Don't waste money on new teeth." Although Coleman ate well, he was not an amiable companion. "People here are crazy. I can't understand what they say," he said loudly at lunch, then asked, "What kind of restaurant is this? Let's go to a different one." When he finished eating, Coleman demanded to go to bed. Once when a nurse said she would help him into bed in five minutes, he shouted, "Shit! Do you want me to crawl out of this restaurant onto the street and get run over by a car!"

I sat in Coleman's room while he dozed. When he awoke, I gave him candy. Usually he gummed two pieces, then fell back to sleep. To pass time I looked at pictures on the wall. Coleman's roommate fought in World War II. The Japanese captured him in the Philippines, and he endured the Bataan Death March and then three and a half years in prisoner of war camps. Unable to walk or talk, the man was again a prisoner, suffering through another death march. One afternoon while I sat in the room, I heard a woman shout, "Please send me back! Please send me back!" "Back where?" I wondered. "Perhaps back through fancy to that far country Youth," I speculated. Occasionally while Coleman slept I wandered community rooms in the home. Old people rocked incessantly, the chairs shaking but going nowhere. Although their lives were diminished, the patients did not seem pitiful. "Mother," Coleman said, "expected too much of us." In the rooms I did not see sadness or heartbreak but reality. Maybe people should not expect too much of life itself. "Winter will come to you," Slubey Garts said, "just as it comes to the young grasshopper sitting on a sweet potato vine." One morning when I mentioned Vanderbilt, Coleman immediately quoted part of the first stanza of Robert Browning's "Rabbi Ben Ezra": "Grow old along with me! / The best is yet to be, / The last of life, for which the first was made." The poem was one of Father's favorites, and when Coleman broke down, I recited the rest of the stanza: "Our times are in his hand / Who saith, 'A whole I planned; / Youth shows but half. Trust God; see all, / nor be afraid!'" When I finished, I gave Coleman a piece of candy, and he tumbled into sleep.

My flight back to Hartford left Houston at seven in the morning. I don't trust wake-up calls, so the night before leaving Texas I didn't sleep. At 3:30 I dressed and checked out of the motel. At 4:30 I left the interstate highway near Hobby Airport. Although I smelled airplane fuel, I couldn't find the airport, so I bought gas and asked directions. Alas, I still couldn't find the terminal, so I drove to another gas station. The attendant sat in a box surrounded by bars and bullet-proof glass. A drunk slumped against a pump, raking through his wallet and scattering paper across the asphalt. I did not want to linger about the station, so I jumped out of the car, leaving the keys in the ignition, lights on, air-conditioning and motor running. As I bent over to speak to the attendant, I heard a click. The car door had shut and locked. I wore a blue and yellow sports coat. Tailored by Gordon of Philadelphia and sold by Davison's at Sea Island, Georgia, the coat smacked of soft privilege, not the hard living endemic to South Houston. The only bright thing on the block, I looked like a Christmas tree, one decorated, I feared, with ornaments for the taking. I asked the attendant to let me join him in the box. "I can't let you in," he said. "Here's ten dollars," I said, "the price of admission and a phone call." At five o'clock I telephoned Avis at the airport. Ten minutes later two men arrived in a van and unlocked the door. I followed them to the airport, driving with my head out the car window, the air-conditioning having fogged up the windshield and the switch for the wiper obscure amid a jumble of knobs and buttons.

Turbulence terrifies me, and I cannot sleep on airplanes. To smooth the buck out of flying, I corral nouns and verbs and break them to sentence and paragraph. In Houston I saw a book entitled *Growing Up Jewish*. In Storrs I had seen books with similar titles: Growing Up Lesbian, Estonian, Purple, and Manic Depressive. None of the books described my childhood, and on the plane I sketched an essay called "Growing Up Episcopalian." In one book a colon appeared in the title followed by the phrase "Searching for the Pain." Growing up Episcopalian is a painless experience. Although problems facing Episcopal youth may cause anxiety, they rarely ache or bleed, being matters such as mastering the sand wedge, overcoming a wobble in the backhand, and choosing the right fork at the country club. Wacky dietary restrictions don't give Episcopalians colitis. Episcopalians can eat anything so long as they do so with good manners. Moreover, the Episcopalian does not bind his head in a cummerbund or jab studs through his nostrils. Once the Episcopalian masters the art of wearing regimental ties, preferably those with blue and red stripes running right to left, he is free to adorn himself with the blowzy and the artificial: yellow and blue sports coats, even red trousers and saddle shoes. If boxers flutter below the legs of his shorts on hot days, as mine do, the Episcopalian merely thinks the ruffles decorative. Because Episcopalians ignore doctrine, they never suffer from religious melancholia. Members of elevated Episcopal churches are occasionally exceptions to this rule, however. The higher the church, the lower the people. People who genuflected, Mother used to say, were jumped-up Druids and were not to be trusted on any social occasion superior to a Brownie bake sale. Only once have I heard of an Episcopalian's being accused of heresy. At a vestry meeting at St. Mark's in Nashville, Caldworth Wentwell shouted, "there is no stock market!" After Caldworth pleaded diminished responsibility because of martinis and pledged to endow a putting green at the Home for Impecunious Suffragan Brokers, the charge was dropped.

The woman sitting next to me on the plane asked what I was writing. On my telling her, she said, "Go for it." She was a Baptist and did not know that the Episcopalian rarely goes for anything. Instead, he lets *it* come to him. Not all the world, however, is oyster to the youthful Episcopalian. Some occupations resemble tainted mussels. Much as a Christian Scientist rarely becomes a proctologist, so Episcopal parents encourage their progeny to avoid not only political and military shenanigans but also the whole dotty asylum of therapists and counselors.

Episcopalians are not opinionated. They realize that opinion is a creature of whim, in contrast to manners. Not believing in absolutes, Episcopalians are masters of light conversation. Because they know words live only in the moment, Episcopalians are free to be willful and to say whatever they wish. "Shitass!" Mother exclaimed at dinner one Sunday after church as she passed me a drumstick. "The Wardells are shitasses." Episcopalians make poor patriots. "The appeal to patriotism is an appeal to prejudice," I heard a bishop say, "all right for covens of snakehandlers and foot washers, sects for whom reason is no more than a trembling in the liver." Because Episcopalians believe in nothing absolutely, they are sure of their actions. Years ago a woman who worked for my family told Mother that her furniture was being repossessed because she had missed two payments. On asking how long the woman had paid for the furniture, Mother learned that the payments had stretched through years. That afternoon Mother visited the merchant. When she left the store, not only did she hold a receipt marked "Paid," but the merchant opened the door for her. The next day a truck delivered a reclining chair to the woman.

Episcopalians are remarkably capable. If an Episcopalian sees a dog dropping on the floor, he bends over and picks it up. In this life at least, Episcopalians forswear the affectation of towelettes and pooper scoopers. "What about sex?" the woman next to me asked. "For hormonal Episcopalians there are two classes of people, those with whom one cavorts and those with whom one does not cavort but whom one eventually marries." "I must add," I continued as the woman looked puzzled, "that an Episcopalian does not define cavorting, or sashaying for that matter. Either activity could include any number of pleasantries. Moreover, the Episcopalian is free to decorate house with a friend of the same sex, just so long as the friend is presentable." "Good Lord!" the woman exclaimed. "Amen," I responded, closing my notebook and the conversation because the plane had begun its descent into Hartford.

When I got back to Storrs, Vicki was at the grocery, and the children were in school. The afternoon was bright, and I decided to roam the woods. Coreopsis and ox-eyed daisies spotted a bank. Crowns of pale orange flowers circled English plantain. Butterflies bloomed like flowers. While a cloudy wing clung to red clover, cabbage whites and yellow swallowtails puddled on a road, the swallowtails trembling slightly, the whites jumping nervously. Fragrance melted from multiflora rose, turning breezes pink and purple. Perfume slipped from a pillow of sweet-scented bedstraw and blew through the air in feathers. In the marsh at the foot of the ski tow, dragonflies skittered across vision like wafers. Under a board a milk snake curled in a hand, its skin a glove of red saddles trimmed with black, yellow, and gray.

Blossoms hung on swamp rose like lavender broaches. Below the beaver dam forget-me-nots wound through grass in bracelets. On laurel, buds resembled cake decorations, pushed white and creamy out of a sleeve. In the Ogushwitz meadow green bundles of buds hung lumpy from milkweed, ladybugs scurrying over them like sales girls in department stores. This spring the Fenton River flooded and sprayed sand across the meadow. For the first time green dragon appeared. Leaves swirled above stalks in blades. Curving out from spathes, the tongues of dragons flickered, tasting the air. By the beaver pond reed canary grass shined, its anthers yellow as banners. Tassels hung nonchalantly from fringed sedge while blossoms burst raucous from the side of soft rush. A yellow throat hopped tut-tutting through alders. In the woods behind the pond verries sang, their songs incessant, turning like screws, almost as if they were trying to buckle permanence to season. In the background wrens jittered nervously, and vireos called "over hear."

When I returned home from the woods, Vicki told me Eliza was playing soccer at Spring Hill. I hurried to the field. Eliza was sweeper. She had played the whole game and was tired. When she remained close to her goal while her team pushed up the field, I urged her to pick up the pace. Eliza stopped in midstride, and turning toward me, put her hands on her hips, and shouted, "Mr. Pickering, the coach is on the other side of the field. She is a she, not a he or a you." Parents along the sidelines winced nervously. "Youth is something," Chuck said. "Yes," I answered, then thinking of Houston, added, "so is old age." Unaccountably I started singing to myself. "The sun shines bright in the old Kentucky home, / 'Tis summer, the darkies are gay, / The corn-top's ripe and the meadow's in bloom, / While the birds make music all the day." Nostalgia for vanished springs clung to the old home like ivy. "The day goes by like a shadow o'er the heart, / With sorrow where all was delight," I muttered, feeling both joyful and sad, joyful to see Eliza my beautiful dreamer running through the green day, sad because I knew that both the grass and the "queen of my song" would eventually wither.

For Coleman my visit accomplished little. In contrast the trip made me appreciate the glimmering moments of my life. The game was almost over when I arrived. "What are you singing?" Eliza said when she walked off the field. "My favorite songs by Stephen Foster," I answered, putting my arm over her shoulders. "I haven't thought about them for a long time," I added, singing, "I dream of Eliza, with the light brown hair, / Borne, like a vapor on the summer air; / I see her tripping where the bright streams play, / Happy as the daisies, that dance on her way." "Did you have a good trip to Houston?" Eliza asked. "I had a wonderful trip," I said. "Let's go home."